GARDEN AND AVIARY BIRDS OF INDIA

GARDEN AND AVIARY BIRDS OF INDIA

FRANK FINN, B.A., F.Z.S., M.B.O.U.

WITH SEVEN FULL PAGE ILLUSTRATIONS

GYAN

Published by

Gyan Publishing House
5, Ansari Road
Daryaganj, New Delhi-110002
Phone: 011-47034999, 9811692060
E-mail: books@gyanbooks.com

Distribution Network
gyanbooks.com
India, USA, Canada, UK, Australia, France

ISBN: 978-81-212-9286-3 (PB)
First Published, 1915

2nd Impression 2023

Printed at: Gyan Press, Delhi.

GARDEN AND AVIARY BIRDS OF INDIA

Author: FRANK FINN

PLATE I.

One-half Natural Size.

1.—COPPERSMITH (Green; scarlet forehead and breast, yellow face and throat). 2.—PARADISE FLY-CATCHER (White with black head and blue bill). 3.—AVADAVAT (Red with white spots). 4.—MAGPIE ROBIN OR DHYAL (Black and white). 5.—SCARLET-BACKED FLOWER-PECKER (Black, cream and scarlet).

GARDEN AND AVIARY BIRDS OF INDIA

BY

FRANK FINN, B.A., F.Z.S., M.B.O.U.

WITH SEVEN FULL-PAGE ILLUSTRATIONS

SECOND EDITION

CALCUTTA

THACKER, SPINK AND CO

1915

TO MY FRIEND,

RAI R. B. SANYAL, BAHADUR, C.M.Z.S.,

Superintendent of the Calcutta Zoo,

I DEDICATE THIS BOOK.

PREFACE.

ANGLO-INDIAN readers of the present work will notice that birds of prey, waders, game-birds and water-fowls have been omitted therefrom, although some species of these—such as the kite—are among the very commonest birds of the East; but this was done owing to exigencies of space, which compelled greater attention to some of the "small birds." In dealing with these, also, I have endeavoured, where a choice had to be made, to deal with as many different groups as possible, rather than to particularize many species in one group, in the hope of making the book serviceable as an introduction to the study of the ornithology of our Eastern Empire.

The same considerations have guided me in the avicultural part of the work, wherein I have endeavoured to meet the requirements of the beginner in bird-keeping by indicating those species which are most easily obtained and kept. The names of imported cage-birds are distinguished by an asterisk in the letter press and by Italics in the List of Contents.

F. FINN.

LONDON, 1915.

CONTENTS.

Note.—Names of birds not occurring wild in the Indian Empire are given above in italics, while in the text they are marked with an asterisk.

LIST OF ILLUSTRATIONS.

GARDEN AND AVIARY BIRDS
OF INDIA.

CHAPTER I.

CLASSIFICATION AND BOOKS OF REFERENCE.

FOR the purposes of the present work, I shall not usually discuss the various orders of birds, but shall confine myself to families, as the limits of these are very well defined and generally agreed upon by ornithologists, while with regard to the orders hardly any two books agree. The scientific names employed will be those of the bird volumes of the *Fauna of British India* for Indian Birds; while for the foreign species which I shall have occasion to deal with I shall use those of the *British Museum Catalogue of Birds.* Names of birds not occurring wild in the Indian Empire are marked with an asterisk.

And here a few words on the subject of the classificatory terms employed by naturalists may not be out of place, as they are not always understood by beginners.

A *species* is a collection of individuals which reproduce others like themselves. Thus, over most of India we find numbers of green Parrots with long, pointed tails, and if we watch the domestic affairs of these we shall discover that their young, as a rule, preserve the same type. All these birds, therefore, we group as a species, called in English the Rose-ringed Parrakeet, from the pink ring on the neck of the males. In some places we shall come across a smaller Parrakeet, of the same general shape, but with the head of a strikingly different colour from the body—plum-colour in the male and dull purple in the female. If we attend to the propagation of these we shall discover that their young in turn resemble them, although the coloured head takes some time to develop. These, then, form another species, called the Plum-headed Parrakeet.

Further research will show us yet other kinds, all agreeing in general shape, but differing slightly in proportions, and more in colour. We group all these together as a *genus;* in popular language, they are all birds of the same *style*, though each species, or collection of individuals, differs in certain details which are peculiar to it.

If we examine the Parrakeets brought from Australia, we shall observe that while they can be divided up into groups of individuals, forming species, which groups differ in colour even more strikingly than our Indian birds, yet many of them agree closely in certain details which mark them off as another group or genus. Thus, though their tails are long and pointed, they are very much shorter and broader than those of the Indian Parrakeets; their legs are longer, and, if we come to keep and observe them, we shall find their movements are rather different. So we say they are birds of another genus or style.

Yet it is perfectly obvious that both of these collections of species have much in common—there is a *family* resemblance between them, as we say. Hence, the Indian green long-tailed Parrakeets, and the Australian many-coloured broad-tailed Parrakeets, are both said to belong to the family *Psittacidæ*.

The classical name is used in order to make our books intelligible to naturalists all over the world, who may not know our particular language. So, also, we use a special word, compounded from two Greek ones to express the long-tailed green Parrakeets of India—*Palæornis*. This means "the bird of old," these Parrots having been the first known to the ancients, who called them by the name *Psittacus*, which means Parrot. The word *Psittacidæ* means "the family of *Psittacus*"—the Parrot clan, so to speak.

The Australian branch of the clan is also designated by a compound Greek name—*Platycercus*, meaning "broad-tailed." This name is of course of modern invention, though on classical lines.

In order to designate the species, a specific name, generally Latin, is tacked on to the name of the genus. Thus, the Rose-ringed Parrakeet is called *Palæornis torquatus*, *torquatus* meaning "ringed." The plum-headed is called *Palæornis cyanocephalus*, *cyanocephalus* (which happens to be Greek) meaning blue-headed.

Similarly, the most familiar species of broad-tailed Australian Parrakeet, known in English as the Rosella, is called in scientific language *Platycercus eximius*, *eximius* being a Latin word meaning "excellent," on account of the striking beauty of this showy bird.

In commencing this subject, I mentioned that individuals of a species *usually* produced young like themselves. But they do not *always* do so; the Ring-necked Parrakeet, for instance, not unfrequently produces a yellow young bird, quite different from its ordinary green offspring. Such an individual is said to belong to a *variety* of the species; it came from green parents, and for all we know, may, if it has the chance, produce green young in its turn—may " throw back, " as breeders say.

If, however, common green Parrakeets never produced yellow young, and if in a certain district, *all* the Parrakeets of a certain *Palæornis* type were yellow, we should call this a species; it would probably be known as *Palæornis luteus*, *luteus* being the Latin for " yellow." We should presume that these birds were the offspring of yellow parents, and would in their turn produce yellow young—would "breed true," as is commonly said.

Every variety, therefore, has a chance of becoming a species, and every species must have once been a variety, if the theory of the evolution of species from pre-existing species be admitted, as it is generally now-a-day

It will thus be seen that the distinction between species and variety is a piece of zoological snobbery, so to speak; if a bird's antecedents are all right and a likeness has been handed down from father to son indefinitely, as far as we can see, he belongs to a " good species:" but if he is convicted of having sprung from parents unlike himself, he is a mere *parvenu*, stigmatized as a "variety," "aberration," or "sport."

Of course, such varieties have often been fixed by breeding from them in captivity, as we shall see later ; and the work of bird-fanciers and stock-breeders in this direction has been of an importance which has never yet received its due meed of praise and encouragement, considering that by studying it Darwin was able to demonstrate the possibility of the production of one form from another, and thus to raise the study of zoology from a mere pastime to a philosophy of life.

The name descriptive of the particular *species* is, it will be seen, placed under that of the *genus*, although the opposite obtains in English and Hindustani. This is simply because in Latin the adjective always follows the substantive, as in so many other languages ; and all scientific nomenclature follows the rules of Latin Grammar, although the words are more often than not adopted from the Greek. Besides which, it is certainly a great convenience to have the generic name first, just as in indexing a number of people's names one reverses the usual order and puts the surname before the Christian name.

If we carry our investigations into Parrots further, we shall find a number of species, grouped again into generations which differ very much from the Indian long-tails and Australian broad-tails. They have brush-tipped tongues, run a great deal to red in colour, have a peculiar smell, a sharp cry, and live on soft food, not on grain.

They are, we may say, quite a different family altogether, and we give them a different family name, the Lories (*Lorūdæ*). This, of course, means the family of *Lorius*, the native name *Lori* turned into Latin as the Romans would have done it, if they had ever seen a Lory.

But still the Lories are obviously Parrots of a sort, and so we group their family, and the other family of *Psittacidæ*, together, and call the whole collection the *order* of Parrots (*Psittaci*).

Thus, a collection of similar individuals make a *species*; collections of species, having a great deal in common but differing in details, make a *genus*; collections of genera bearing a certain resemblance, make a *family*; and collections of families also agreeing in certain important points, make an *order*.

The various orders in conjunction with each other make up the *class* of birds, which may be at once defined as feathered animals, no other creature living or extinct possessing feathers. A bony skeleton is shared by birds with beasts, reptiles, and fishes, and in their general anatomy they approach reptiles more closely than any other class of backboned animals; it will be remembered also that reptiles, on their part, lay eggs like birds.

I shall conclude this chapter with a list of works of reference for those who may wish to go further into the subject than I am here taking them.

For the general subject of classification, anatomy, &c., the best books are Professor A. Newton's Dictionary of Birds, and Mr. F. E. Beddard's Structure and Classification of Birds

For Indian Birds, the Fauna of British India, the four volumes dealing with birds. Dr. Jerdon's Birds of India is admirable, but out of print. Of the British Museum Catalogue of Birds, Volume XX, by Count T. Salvadori, which treats of the Parrots of the world, will be most useful. For the management of many foreign species beyond those which are mentioned here, Dr. A. G. Butler's *Foreign Finches in Captivity*, and *Foreign Bird-keeping* may be profitably consulted.

CHAPTER II.

PASSERINE BIRDS.

THE CROWS, BABBLERS, AND BULBULS.

MORE than half of the known species of birds belong to the great Passerine order, so called from the Latin name of its most prominent member, *Passer*, the Sparrow. Birds of this order are usually small, the Raven being the biggest, while some are almost the smallest of birds. The Sparrow and Mynah represent fair average sizes of Passerine birds.

They can always be distinguished by their feet; the foot of a Sparrow or Crow will serve as a model for all. The shank is slight, and covered behind with long entire plates, and before with a single row of large broad scales, or even with one continuous horny plate; there are three toes before, unconnected by any web or other junction and one behind, which, taking it with its claw, is as big as or bigger than any of the rest.

The shank may be long or short, and the foot as a whole large or small as compared with the bird's body, but the style of scaling and proportion of the toes is always unmistakeable. The shape, and the wings, tail, and beak vary a great deal in Passerine birds; but they always have large heads in proportion to their size.

Their young are always hatched blind, helpless, and naked or nearly so; their nests are usally in a bush or tree, and they live in pairs in the breeding season. They are the most skilful nest-builders of all birds, and the only ones which are commonly accounted songsters. They bear captivity well, but are not so easy to breed in that state as some groups of birds.

The order is divided into many families, which are not always easy to distinguish, as there are many connecting links.

THE CROWS.

Birds of the Crow family are usually of a fair size; they have stout bills, garnished with bristly feathers at the root, as may be easily seen in our old friend, the House-Crow. Mail and female are alike, and the young only differ in being duller.

That grey-headed scoundrel, the House-Crow (*Corvus splendens*), and the "big black bounding beggar," his jungle relative (*Corvus macrorhynchus*) need mention only to be condemned. They will insist on one's studying their habits, on account of their appalling propensity for mischief; and for this reason, and because of the fact that they are deadly enemies to the eggs and young of all birds weaker than themselves, they should be banished by all possible means from every bird-lover's garden.

The Magpies, however, are of a better *jat.* They have shorter wings, though longer tails, than Crows and are smaller in size; so, with the best will in the world to commit it, they cannot get through the same amount of mischief, while they are singularly ornamental.

THE COMMON INDIAN MAGPIE OR WANDERING TREEPIE (*Dendrocitta rufa*) is well known as *Handichancha* or *Kotree* to the natives of Bengal. This pretty bird is a familiar garden visitor, and his short wings and long tail make him conspicuous in his easy dipping flight. His colour is also unmistakeable, being buff or cinnamon with a sooty head and grey, black-tipped wings and tail. He is an omnivorous feeder, and has been accused of destructiveness to garden produce, but as he certainly devours large numbers of insects, and also acts as a check on the undue increase of small birds, he probably does more good than harm. His notes are often very pretty, and when taken young, he can be taught to speak,—a common accomplishment in the Crow family.

Hardly ever you will see him n the ground, and when there he can only hop, not walking like the pied Magpie at home.

The nest is built high up in a tree, and is open or cup-shaped, as usual in this family; the eggs, which are spotted, vary from pinkish to greenish in ground colour.

This bird is one of our commonest Indian species, being found throughout India and Burma in the plains, and ascending the hills up to 7,000 feet. The hill climate appears to agree with it, as hill birds are the largest in size.

The bird ordinarily measures about a foot and a half, of which a foot is taken up by the tail.

THE RED-BILLED BLUE MAGPIE (*Urocissa occipitalis*) is a splendid creature possessing a tail half-a-yard long, with a body about the size of the House-Crows. In colour the Blue Pie is a rich purple blue with the head and neck jet black and the bill and feet scarlet. There is a white patch at the back of the head, and the wings and tail are tipped with white. The belly is also white, but with a strong tinge of blue. On the whole this is certainly the most beautiful member of the Crow family found in any country. I have never seen this bird except in captivity, but even so, its appearance is so striking that I can sympathize with the great admiration expressed by those friends of mine who have seen it flying at large. In the Indian hills it ranges from five thousand feet to a considerably higher elevation, being common near some of our stations; but in Burma, where it is also found, it inhabits the plains as well. It is constantly brought down to Calcutta in the winter and does well in captivity there. Specimens can be bought at the proper season for about ten rupees or less; and a few have reached Europe, where they would probably do well out doors in mild climates.

The bird is known as *Nilkhant* at Mussoorie and *Diggdall* at Simla. It builds at varying heights; the nest is open, but the eggs are greenish with brown spots like the English Magpie's.

The so-called Australian Magpie is really a shrike, and will be described under that heading. It is commonly imported. The bird usually called the Blue-Jay in India, is also wrongly named, being really a Roller: it will be dealt with in its turn. Meanwhile it may be mentioned that the real Jays are well represented in our hills. They are birds with moderately long tails like Crows, but short wings like Magpies. Like the Magpies also, they are very ornamental, and rather useful than harmful. Most of them have a strong general resemblance to the English Jay, but one common species is very distinct and striking.

THE BLACK-HEADED JAY (*Garrulus lanceolatus*), is called *Ban-sarrah* by the Simla hill-men. I saw it commonly about Mussoorie. It is about the size of a pigeon, of a delicate pinkish-drab, with black head, and wings and tail most beautifully barred with black and blue, and tipped with white. It is a showy bird, exposing itself freely and often playing on the wing above the trees. It is found all over the Himalayas, ranging to 8,000 feet in summer, and coming as low down as Dehra in winter. It builds an open nest in medium-sized trees and lays greenish-white eggs with brown spots. Some birds are brought down alive to Calcutta every winter.

Magpies and Jays make the best of aviary birds; for cages they are too large and dirty. They can be kept together, and with other birds well able to take care of themselves, such as the larger Mynahs and Babblers; small birds they would eat without compunction. They should, indeed, always have some raw animal food, as noted in the final chapter on management. Fruit is also needful; but almost any cooked food will do as the daily diet for these omnivorous birds, and an aviary can be kept going on house scraps. Inch-mesh wire-netting will be suitable for birds of this size, and any mice or sparrows that get through will stand an excellent chance of never getting out again. Care should be taken that they do not stow away enough of their food to let it get offensive; for they are of provident habits and will hide away scraps as readily as a dog. Worthless objects are also secreted with care; a pair of Blue Magpies at the Calcutta Zoo some years ago used to amuse us much by their methodical way of folding pieces of paper and putting them away.

THE TITS.

The Tits are now-a-days classed near the Crows, and in many of their habits may be called Jays in miniature. They resemble Jays in shape, though not so big as Sparrows; male and female are alike, and the young only a little duller; and the nostrils are covered at the root with bristles, as in the Crows. Tits are as omnivorous in their way as Crows are, and have the same tricks of holding down their food with their feet, and of storing away superfluities. But they usually build in holes, unlike most of the Crow tribe. Most of the Tits in India are hill-birds, and will be recognized as a group by many people, the family being so familar at home. Almost all the *species* are different, however; here there is only room to allude to two.

The Yellow-cheeked Tit (*Machlolophus xanthogenys*) is a thick-set little bird about five inches long with a full crest, black throat, and yellow face and breast, the latter marked with a black central streak; the back is olive-green and the wings and tail slaty-grey.

This bird is found throughout the Himalayas at moderate elevations and breeds in April and May, laying four or five red-spotted white eggs in a hole. It is the only Tit I have seen in confinement here, several having been brought down to Calcutta of late years. It does well as a captive, and from its beauty and active movements is a nice pet. But it should not be trusted with birds no larger than itself, as it has murderous proclivities, like Tits in general—another proof of their relationship to the blackguard Crow. Tits in confinement should have hemp-seed and cracked nuts in addition to the usual food of small insectivorous birds. Cocoanut shells should be provided for them to sleep in, and two, even of the same species, should not be put together without great caution.

The Indian Grey Tit (*Parus atriceps*), called in Bengali *Ram-gangra*, is grey above and dirty white below; the head and breast, with a streak running down from the latter, are black except for the pure white cheeks Young birds have a strong yellow tinge throughout the plumage. This bird is a little smaller than a sparrow; it is the most widely-spread of Indian Tits, being found nearly all over India and Burmah, and frequenting both hills and plains. It breeds from March to June, laying about half-a-dozen eggs, pinky-white with red spots, in any convenient hole in a tree, wall, or even bank. It has a very wide range outside our Empire, being found north to Turkestan and south to the Malay Islands.

THE BABBLERS.

These form the most numerous group of Indian birds and are, of all the smaller fry, the most interesting in my opinion, whether at large or in the aviary.

They vary a good deal in size, but there is something about their general style which marks them off at once when seen in life, though, as skins in a museum collection, they are not so easy to separate. They have very short rounded wings, and rather long tails as a rule; their plumage is lax and fluffy, not close and sleek, and their legs and feet are strong, not to say coarse. Their bills are moderate in size; not actually slender, but not thick like a Crow's. The Peko or Chinese Mocking-bird on Plate III (Fig. 3) will give a good general idea of them, and few are larger than this.

They usually go about in parties, and have a weak flight, never going far at a time, and often whirring and skimming alternately, like Partridges. They feed mostly on insects, and take hold of their food in one foot, if they wish to break it up. On trees or on the ground they are very active, moving about by long hops, for very few of them run. Males and females are alike in colour, and the young remsemble them. They are very affectionate and constantly caress each other with their bills.

THE SAT-BHAI (*Crateropus canorus*) is the most familiar of the larger Babblers, the native name, which of course means seven brothers, having been practically accepted as English. I have not thought it necessary to figure this common bird; everyone must have noticed it, with its pale-drab, dust-coloured plumage, cunning-looking white eyes, and sickly-white legs and bill. It is found all over India in the plains and low down in the hills, and comes freely into gardens, making its presence known obtrusively by a squeaky babbling varied by hysterical outbursts.

In confinement it is very easy to tame, will eat table scraps readily, and is amusing for a time; but nobody would want to keep such a frowsy unmusical creature for long, interesting as its habits undoubtedly are. Birds which I turned out after studying them for some time remained so tame that they would still take food from the hand; and I imagine that a hand-reared one would make a very nice pet. The nest is an open cup-shaped one, placed low down, and the eggs are of a most lovely blue. In Bengal this bird is called *Chataria.*

The Rat-bird (*Argya caudata*) is a less common and smaller species with a long Magpie-like tail, and coloured like a hen-Sparrow. It gets its popular name from the rat-like appearance given by the said tail as it skulks along the ground from bush to bush. This is also a bird of the plains, but not nearly so bold or so common as the *Sat-bhai.* Its nest and eggs are of the same type.

The Streaked Laughing-Thrush (*Trochalopterum lineatum*) is very common in the Himalayas up to 9,000 feet, and is common about houses at Mussoorie.

In shape it resembles the common Babbler of the plains, but is rather smaller. Its plumage is darker, being a streaky mixture of grey and chestnut; the eyes, bill and feet are dark, and the tail has distinct light-grey tips. It is a tame but most uninteresting bird, and has

PLATE II.

One-half Natural Size.

1.—BROWN SHRIKE (Brown, buff below, black eye stripe). 2.—BLACK-HEADED ORIOLE (Black and yellow). 3.—NUTMEG-BIRD (Brown, white and black below). 4.—PIED MYNAH (Black and white).

a feeble note. The eggs are blue, as usual in this group, and the nest low down.

The hills form the home of several large and showy species of this group, often called Jay-Thrushes, a name which well expresses their attributes. The most striking is

THE WHITE-CRESTED LAUGHING-THRUSH (*Garrulax leucolophus*), a bird of nearly the size of a pigeon. In colour it is dark-brown, with the full crest, the neck and breast pure white, and a black mark along each side of the head. The bill and feet are also black. Altogether it reminds one of a lady in evening dress with her hair powdered and wearing a black mask. Its manners, however, although attractive, are not exactly lady-like; for it is a boisterous, rollicking bird, going about in large parties which continuously explode in fits of laughter, the curiously human sound of which is most infectious! In an aviary it keeps up this character, and is a most excellent inmate, although not to be trusted with weak birds, even of its own kind. It inhabits the Himalayas from Gurhwal to Arrakan, but does not range above 6,000 feet. In Pegu and Tenasserim a species with more white on the under-surface takes its place (*Garrulax belangeri*), but the two are much alike. Both lay white eggs in an open nest in a bush.

The Himalayan bird is plentifully brought down to Calcutta in winter, and live specimens can then be easily obtained, together with some other species of large Babblers. All will do well together in an aviary with Magpies, Jays and large Mynahs, and such a collection, if the aviary be large enough, will be found easy to keep and the most picturesque and interesting that could be found. But none of these birds are suited for *small* aviaries.

Only one of the large Babblers has much repute as a songster, and this may almost always be procured in Calcutta.

THE PEKO OR CHINESE MOCKING-BIRD (*Dryonastes Chinensis*) is figured on Plate III, as mentioned on page 15.

This bird is a really fine musician, having singularly pure and plaintive tones; it is also an admirable mimic, and, when tame enough, delights in being caressed. It will live many years in a cage, and is the most easily kept of all the non-seed-eating cage-birds. At the same time it always seems to me a pity not to give this lively and sociable bird the happier life that an aviary affords. It is chiefly known in India as a foreign bird, being imported from China, but it is found in South Pegu and Tenasserim.

Few of the Babblers are as large as most of those I have been describing.

THE BLACK-HEADED SIBIA (*Lioptila capistrata*) is, although nearly nine inches long, a slight, graceful creature; it is figured on Plate IV (Fig. 5). It is a very common bird in the hills up to 8,000 feet, being particularly numerous about Darjeeling. It comes to the ground less than most Babblers, and is fairly strong on the wing; indeed, it is, all round, a most remarkably active bird, and so dexterous that I have seen it turn right round its perch without letting go.

This peculiarity makes it a very nice aviary bird, although it is not brilliant in colour nor particularly tame. It may frequently be obtained from Calcutta dealers during the winter months.

The bird breeds in the hills from May to July, building a cup-shaped nest of moss and fibres, and laying pale green eggs with reddish spots. *Sibya* is its name among the Nepaulese.

THE LIOTHRIX (*Liothrix luteus*) is figured on Plate V (Fig. 4). It is about the size of a Sparrow, and differs strikingly from other members of its family in having a strongly forked tail and particularly smooth and sleek plumage. In addition to the colours mentioned on the plate, the beautiful orange-streaked wings, coral-red bill and black eye make it very easy to recognize.

The males are brighter than the females, sufficiently so to make it no very difficult matter to pick out a pair. This charming little bird is the best known of all Babblers in captivity; many are sold in Calcutta every winter, and many more sent to England; in both cases the birds are usually obtained from China, though the bird is also common all along our hills at 8,000 feet or lower. It is one of the commonest birds about Darjeeling, where its peculiar five-noted call "tee-tee-tee-tee-tee" will probably be heard before the bird is seen, as it is decidedly a skulker.

Dealers usually know it as the China Robin, but although it certainly looks like a Robin, it has a very different disposition and habits. It is a timid, harmless bird, very sociable even with other species and remarkably intelligent. In a cage it is decidedly nervous, but in an aviary becomes very much at home, and shows great inquisitiveness. Many specimens become so tame that they will take food from the fingers when led to the aviary wires. The cock has a very sweet song, very strong for the size of the bird, and altogether it is the most generally attractive small bird I know of—everyone seems to admire it. It is easy to keep for it will eat seed and fruit as well as insects, and therefore, like most omnivorous birds, does well on artificial food. Specimens may be had in Calcutta during the winter months at about two rupees each. In England, it fetches about the same price, and is called the Pekin Robin, or even the "Japanese Nightingale." Although so easy to keep, it does not breed readily in captivity. In a wild state, it builds an open nest in a bush, and lays pale-green eggs with red, brown and purple spots. This would be a most suitable species for acclimatization in all warm temperate climates.

THE BLUE-WINGED SIVA (*Siva cyanuroptera*) is a bird of very similar size, but more elegant form, its tail, which is not forked, being longer. The Siva is of a fawn-brown above, and nearly white below, with beautiful blue wings and tail; the bill is yellowish, and the eyes brown. It has much the same range in our hills as the Liothrix, but is not found out of India. In captivity it is comparatively scarce, and is not quite so easy to keep, not caring about seed. However, it is not by any means a delicate bird. Very few, however, have as yet reached England alive, and it is well worth taking home. In its nesting habits it much resembles the Liothrix.

There are many charming small Babblers in the hills but in the plains few are found. Two, however, need notice here.

THE IORA (*Aegithina tiphia*), called *Shoubiga, Tofik or Fatikjal* by the natives, is a common bird all over the plains, but is not much seen, as it keeps on the trees. Its very sweet, flute-like note, however, often reveals its presence. It is a fluffy, short-tailed little thing, smaller than a Sparrow. The bird figured in the Plate IV (Fig. 4) is a cock in breeding plumage; some are more and others less black than this, according to locality, the Southern Indian birds being the darkest. The hens are simply olive-green above and yellow below, with two white bars on the wing, and the cock in winter also becomes olive-green, but keeps his black wings and tail. Young birds resemble the female. They are occasionally reared by natives in Bengal and kept caged: but they are delicate, although very tame and nice little pets. I have never seen an old bird which had been tamed. The species seems to be altogether an insect-feeder, and hence is not a good subject for captivity. It begins to breed about May, and builds a particularly neat and beautiful little nest, a cup formed of fine fibres and coated outside with cobweb. The eggs are greyish-white marked with brown.

Another small Babbler of the plains though not one of our very commonest birds in the wild state, yet deserves notice, as it makes a most charming cage-bird when hand-reared. This is

THE YELLOW-EYED BABBLER (*Pyctorhis sinensis*), a little creature rather smaller in the body than a Sparrow, but with a long tail Its colour is cinnamon-brown above, and white, shading into buff, below; and it has a stout, curved black bill, and yellow eggs and eyelids. The eyes are also yellow, whence the native name *gulab-chasm.*

This bird is found all over the Empire, but does not ascend the hills to any height; it prefers grass to any other cover, and is less gregarious than most Babblers, going singly or in pairs. It has some very pretty notes, and looks very striking when uttering them with erected head-plumage, the pure white throat looking like a beard. In captivity it is mischievous and quarrelsome; it is not wise to put more than a pair together, or to associate them with birds as small as themselves. Two caged birds of this kind I kept singly were absurdly tame; one would let itself be tickled through the bars with one's finger, and the other could be even taken up in the hand and allowed to fly about, when it would fearlessly explore one's person. I have removed it from my moustache three times in quick succession. Taken altogether, if all Gulab-chasms are anything like these two birds, the species can hardly be excelled as a pet. But, as a true insect-feeder, its food of course will give a little trouble.

It breeds from May to September, building a cup-shaped nest of grass and bark fibre in long grass or a low tree. The eggs are pinkish-white with red blotches.

THE WHITE-EYE OR SPECTACLE BIRD (*Zosterops palpebrosa*) is shown at the top of Plate V (Fig. 2), and is the smallest and most wide-spread of all our Babblers. This little creature is rather of a different build than Babblers generally, having longer wings and shorter tail; but its sociable, cuddlesome habits, and the fact that several small birds which are undoubted Babblers closely approach it, settle its relationship easily enough. The white ring round the eye and the olive-yellow plumage with white belly will easily distinguish it from all other Indian birds. It is found all over India, both on hills and plains; in Burma and China a species or variety with a greener back (*Zosterops simplex*) is also found. This is frequently brought to the Calcutta bazar, where the dealers often try to sell it as a "Humming-bird"! It makes an excellent cage-companion for the little Waxbills, and has a sweet little note of its own. Soft fruit, bread and milk, and small insects are all it requires, and it is so easy to keep that a good many specimens are sent to Europe.

The nest of the Indian variety is most commonly found in April; it may be at any height, and is a very delicate little structure, made of cobwebs and vegetable fibres and suspended like a miniature hammock in a forked twig. Only two eggs are laid, of a pale blue.

THE BULBULS.

The Bulbuls are usually classed as a distinct family from the Babblers, and this arrangement I shall follow here, although, as in the *Fauna of British India*, they come next in order of treatment. Bulbuls are birds of very graceful form and movements; in size they are rather larger than Sparrows; their wings are short but broad, and their tails are long, and nearly even at the tip, instead of being forked or tapering as is usually the case with longish tails. Their bills are rather slight than stout, and of moderate length; their legs are decidedly short. They usually have crests, bushy or pointed, as the case may be. Cock and hen are alike in plumage.

The White-eared Bulbul shown on Plate V (Fig. 3) will give a good general idea of their appearance, and they are all much of the same style, and easy to recognize Usually they have a patch of bright colour under the tail. They are sociable birds, with a graceful, but not rapid flight; they seldom come on the ground, where they look awkward hopping about on their short legs; but on trees and bushes they are lively and active, and quite the most ornamental small birds in India, although their colours are usually sober. They feed mostly on fruit, berries, buds, etc., and are not to be encouraged in a fruit and vegetable garden; but they take insects also, and feed the young on these. They do not hold their food in their feet like Babblers. Their nests are open and made of twigs and fibres and their eggs are usually pink with red spots. One or other species is found all over India, and Africa has many species of its own as well. In captivity they are easy to keep on any soft food and fruit, but unless hand-reared are usually wild and uninteresting, and not at all desirable.

THE COMMON RED-VENTED BULBUL (*Molpastes bengalensis*), is one of the most familiar birds in Calcutta.

This is a largish bird as Bulbuls go, being about nine inches long, and very picturesque in appearance, with its full black crest and black tail tipped with white and set off by a white patch over the root and a crimson one below; the general body colour is drab with light edges, running into jet black on the head and neck. The young birds are more rusty in colour, and have the patch under the tail cinnamon instead of red. When taken from the nest just before they can fly, they are easily reared, and make very nice pets, becoming so tame that they can be left at complete liberty, when they will follow one about. The natives keep this bird for fighting, confined by a soft string tied round the middle of its body. All over India Bulbuls resembling this type, but not quite so large and with black more restricted to the head, are among the commonest birds; and for the purpose of this little work it is not necessary to go into the rather minute distinctions between them.

THE RED-WHISKERED BULBUL is a very striking type of bird, which is found in two species or varieties. Its size is less than that of the dark red-vented Bulbuls, and its back brown, while its underparts are pure white; in Western India there is a dark band across the breast and no white tips to the tail-feathers, while in the Bengal and Burmese birds the white is unbroken, and the tail has white tips. The former species is *Otocompsa fuscicaudata*, and the latter *Otocompsa emeria*. The long black crest, red cheek-patches, and red patch under the tail, which both possess, mark them off at once and make them easily recognizable. Young birds have no red on the cheeks and have buff under the tail where the red will show later.

Where Bulbuls have to be kept away from a garden, it is worth while to keep this species in an aviary, for it is active as well as showy, and sufficiently striking to look well in confinement. The Red-vented Bengal and other dark species look rather dingy when shut up; like so many birds, they only look their best at large.

THE BLACK-CRESTED YELLOW BULBUL (*Otocompsa flaviventris*). This bird has a peak-crest like the last one, and is of about the same size, but very different in colour, having very fluffy plumage of an olive-yellow all over, except the head which is glossy black; the bill and feet are black as in Bulbuls generally, but the eyes, instead of being dark as usual, are bright yellow, which gives the bird a very wicked look. This does not belie its disposition, for it is more quarrelsome than other Bulbuls, although its bill and feet are smaller in proportion, and is apt to bully both its own kind and others. It therefore needs a little looking after, but it is worth some trouble, as it is not only striking in appearance but much tamer than Bulbuls are generally. It is rather widely distributed in India, but local; and only a few specimens turn up from time to time in captivity. Few have been sent to England, so that it is worth taking home. The same consideration applies to

THE WHITE-CHEEKED BULBUL (*Molpastes leucogenys*) which is, however, a common bird along our hills from Murree to Bhutan, up to about 7,000 feet elevation. It is very common and tame in Kashmir, and is known in

Chamba as *Painju*. This bird is, to my taste, the prettiest of all the Bulbuls ; it is nearly eight inches long, and of a drab colour, with a black throat, and lemon-yellow patch under the tail, which appendage is tipped with white ; there is also a white patch on each side of the face. The eyes are large and dark, and the crest full, with each feather pointed and gracefully curled up. It is not particularly tame in confinement, unfortunately, but its beauty renders it a very desirable bird where it can be viewed at close quarters. I should think, also, that being a hill-bird it would be particularly suitable to any one who would like on retiring to keep Bulbuls in a garden aviary at home. It might be better called the Curled-crested Bulbul, for its cheeks are not nearly so conspicuously white as those of the next Bulbul on my list.

THE WHITE-EARED BULBUL (*Molpastes leucotis*), called *Bhooroo* in Sindh and *Kushandra* in the Punjab, is figured, as above remarked, on Plate V (Fig. 3), and I need not further describe it, though attention may be drawn to the shortness and bushiness of its crest, and to the rich yellow of the patch under the tail, which is quite of a saffron tint. A bird just like it, but with a much longer and more pointed crest and sulphur yellow under tail-patch, was once got by Mr. Hume at Jalalpoor near Jhelum in the Punjab, and has been described by Mr. Oates as a new species, under the name of *Molpastes humii*. It would be very interesting to get hold of more specimens of this form. for so far only the one is known, and it may perhaps be only a "sport" or variety, though it would not be any the less interesting on that account. The ordinary White-eared

Bulbul has a wide range in the dry north-western and central parts of India, and extends into Persia to the westward. Persian birds are noted to be finer songsters than Indian, and make very nice cage pets. This is, indeed, the nicest cage or aviary bird of all the Bulbuls, being of an unusually tame and friendly disposition even when caught old. It is also unusually intelligent; I remember a bird which I had only had a day or so escaping from its cage and coming back to it the next day. I should say, that a hand-reared bird of this species would be a charming pet, and in any case its tameness and vocal powers strongly recommend it to the fancier. I have never seen it wild, but it may not unfrequently be bought in Calcutta. In confinement, at any rate, it likes to roost at night in a hole instead of perching like most Bulbuls.

THE GREEN BULBULS, or *Harewas*, as they are called by the natives, are classed in the *Fauna of British India* volumes among the Babblers, but Mr. E. C. S. Baker has given good reasons for keeping them among the Bulbuls still. In this I thoroughly agree; these birds have the characteristic short legs of Bulbuls, and they do not use their feet in feeding as Babblers do. However, they are certainly very different in some respects from the typical Bulbuls, though they do not thereby approach the Babblers at all. They have no trace of a crest, their bills are long and curved, and they have a long tongue, which they protrude to suck up liquid food. They are much more active on their feet among the twigs than other Bulbuls, and have a stronger and more vigorous flight.

They are not rare birds, but their colour makes them hard to see among the trees.

THE GOLD-FRONTED HAREWA (*Chloropsis aurifrons*) is the best known of them all; it has a wide range through the sub-Himalayan tracts, Eastern Bengal, and Burma, extending to Cambodia. Moreover, it is often caged, and may commonly be bought in Calcutta. The figure (Fig. 5) on Plate V will give an idea of its general form, but its beautiful colouring must be seen to be appreciated. The grass-green of the body is most beautifully set off by the brilliant orange forehead and purple-blue throat, the latter surrounded by a black bib or gorget. At the bend of the wing is a patch of shining turquoise-blue, which, however, is only to be seen when the bird is excited. The whole plumage, though close and sleek, is wonderfully fluffy and abundant. Cock and hen are alike, but the young have no black or orange about the head and hardly any blue, being practically green all over.

The Harewa is one of those birds which universally attract a well-deserved admiration. The specimens offered for sale are often hand-reared, and then are most charmingly tame, advancing and pecking gently at one's finger without the slightest fear, and even when turned loose in an aviary, they retain this pleasant familiarity and always come up for notice. They will do well in a cage, but of course better still in a large space, and their feeding presents no great difficulty, as long as it be remembered that the food should be soft. Bread-and-milk sop, milk puddings and soft fruit such as plantain, custard-apple and papya, is quite sufficient for them, with the daily addition of a few insects. Moreover, in addition to its beauty, the Harewa has the recommendation of being a songster, with great powers of mimicry; Mr. Rutledge told me he knew of one which could render the song of the Nightingale perfectly. There is one drawback, however, to this lovely bird, and that is its very savage temper in some cases. In the wild stage Mr. Baker has seen two of these birds fight to death, and another couple defy law and order by hustling a King-Crow, of all birds! And in confinement it is difficult to get two to live together; while some specimens are perfectly impossible companions for other small birds, savagely driving them about and not allowing them to feed. Many individuals, however, are quite peaceable with other birds, and a true pair will live together in harmony.

CHAPTER III.

PASSERINE BIRDS—*continued.*
SHRIKES, MYNAHS, ORIOLES, &c.

THE DRONGOS.

THIS small family stand very much by themselves in most classifications, but there can be little doubt that they are simply peculiar-looking Shrikes. and I put them here simply out of deference to the order followed in the *Fauna of British India* bird volumes, where they are given family rank as usual. Certainly no one can mistake a Drongo for any other Shrike or small bird of any kind, the usually jet-black plumage and long-forked tail making it conspicuous at once. The bill is strong and rather like a Crow's on a small scale, and the legs and feet short but powerful and sharply clawed. The wings are of medium length, and the birds though they cannot rival Swallows and such-like birds in the air, are nevertheless very active and graceful flyers, and remarkably clever at aerial evolutions. They feed on insects, and make sallies from a fixed perch, returning to it on completing their capture. If the prey is too big to be swallowed whole, they hold it in one foot, while tearing it into pieces, like many other Shrikes. Both male and female have the same plumage, and the young merely differ in being spotted with white below.

In disposition the Drongos are very different from the sociable birds I have been describing, being fierce and quarrelsome. They usually sit alone, and wage war against intruders whom they disapprove of in a very noticeable way. They build high up in trees, the nest being open and cup-shaped, and the eggs are pale with reddish spots.

There are not many species of Drongos, though they are widely distributed in the warm regions of the Old World, and here it will only be necessary to deal with two of them.

THE KING-CROW (*Dicrurus ater*) is, with his jet-black plumage and forked tail, one of the most familiar and conspicuous of Indian birds, and rejoices in a number of native names. Thus in Bengal he is called *Finga*, in Southern India, *Buchanga*, and in the Deccan, most appropriately, *Kotwal*. For he certainly acts the part of a police-officer among the birds, being, in spite of his small size (for although he is a foot long, half of this is tail), a terror to kites and crows, and exercising a general supervision over the feathered community. All over India in the plains and up to 5,000 feet in the hills, the King-Crow exerts his sway, and he must bless the English Government for providing him with telegraph wires to sit on and act as overseer in comfort. Nevertheless, he is more adaptable than other Drongos, which seem never to come to the ground, and if there is not a tree, wire, fence, post, cow, or sheep to sit on, he will sit about on *terra-firma* and look out for the grasshoppers, &c., which form his food. It may be this readiness to make the best of things which has given him such a wide range, for he is found all through Africa south of the Sahara and east of India and Burma he goes to Southern China. He is not a songster, but some of his notes are very pleasant; he begins them at daybreak before most birds, although he is at the same time very late in going to roost.

The hens of the species are remarkable for laying eggs of two quite different types, either pale salmon-colour with brownish-red spots or pure white without any spots at all. I presume the white spotting, which certainly distinguishes the young birds, must appear after they leave the nest, for I never saw a nestling with it.

Although it would be cruel and absurd to cage so active and common a bird as this, especially as his habits render him an undesirable companion for other species, yet a hand-reared nestling King-Crow would probably make a very nice pet to fly about at large, and would protect the young poultry by driving off the crows and kites.

THE BHIMRAJ OR RACKET-TAILED DRONGO (*Dissemurus paradiseus*).—This is the only one member of the *Drongo* family which is at all commonly kept in confinement and it is certainly a most interesting pet. It is about twice as large as the King-Crow, with a strong crow-like bill, a crest of narrow feathers rising from the forehead and gracefully curving back, a ruff of hackles round the neck, and each outer tail-feather of a remarkable length, up to more than a foot and a half. Most of this is bare shaft, there being only about a couple of inches of webbing at the tip, like a tassel. The rest of the tail is of quite ordinary length, less than seven inches long. The big side-streamers are not fully developed the first season, and, of course, are usually broken off in the miserable little cages in which these poor birds are usually kept.

The plumage of the Bhimraj is of the usual Drongo blue-black, young birds having a few white spots under the wing. The bill and feet are also black; but once I saw in Mr. Rutledge's possession a most curious variety which had an ivory-white beak, contrasting very well with the black plumage. The only other sign of albinism the bird showed was that some of its secondary wing-feathers and its two hind-claws were also white. White claws and white feathers are not so very uncommon among these birds, I fancy; but I never saw any such variation in the humbler King-Crow, though Mr. B. B. Osmaston once showed me the two wings of an ash-grey specimen of the latter bird which he had shot.

The Bhimraj is found over a large part of India and extends east through Burma to the Malay Peninsula. It is a jungle-haunting bird, and more sociable than Drongos generally. Mr. Oates states that it is probably the finest song-bird in the East. In confinement it is very friendly and fond of notice, and the best of all pet birds. But it *must* have a large cage—about three feet square—and plenty of live insects, or it will not thrive long. It is well worth taking trouble over, as it is a most perfect mimic, giving the cries and songs of all sort of birds and other animals, whistling tunes perfectly, and occasionally even talking. It is a very good aviary bird if kept along with such birds as Jays, large Babblers, &c., for it is too predatory in disposition to be trusted with birds smaller than itself. Taken altogether, there is hardly any bird more interesting to the fancier.

THE WARBLERS.

The Warblers form a very numerous family of birds, spread all over the Old World. More than a hundred are found in our Empire either as residents or winter visitors, but as they are insignificant little birds, generally smaller than sparrows, and of a plain olive-green or brown in colour, they do not attract attention, especially as they keep close in the trees and bushes, searching for insects on which they live. One of our resident Warblers is, however, an exception, being a very noticeable and well-known bird.

THE TAILOR-BIRD (*Orthotomus sutorius*), called *Phutki* in Hindustani and *Tuntuni* in Bengali, is at home in every garden as well as in low jungles and bushy grass-land all over India, Ceylon, and Burma; it ranges east to Siam and China, but does not go more than 4,000 feet up the Himalayas. The figure on Plate IV (Fig. 3) will give a good idea of the male in his summer or breeding plumage. After the breeding season his tail becomes shorn of its long feathers, and is then shorter than his body instead of longer, as the hen's always is. Both have the same colour; but the plumage of the young is slightly duller, and the chestnut cap barely indicated in them.

Many Warblers are good songsters, but the Tailor-bird is not one of these; he has, however, an astonishingly loud call-note, "*to-whit, to-whit,*" which draws attention to him at once. Also although his wings are short and weak he is not at all shy or skulking in habits, so that he is really a conspicuous little bird as he hops about the bushes or on the ground with his tail cocked up perpendicularly. He is a useful little insect destroyer, and has long been famed for his skill in nest-building. Fixing upon a big leaf, or two or three growing close together if one is not enough, he makes a cup or case by putting the edges of the leaf or leaves together, actually sewing them into place, by thread passed through holes bored by his bill. The thread is usually cocoon-silk, but the bird will steal cotton ends if he can get them. Exactly how this remarkable sewing feat is done does not appear to be recorded, and the birds are so wary that though I have lived for some years in a compound where they breed, I have not even seen the nest *in situ*, much less observed their way of working. Inside the leaf-cup is made a little nest of plant-down, hair, &c., and three or four tiny eggs, spotted with red on a reddish-white or bluish-green ground, are laid in it.

The young Tailor-birds when fledged and out of the nest, are very tame. I have not succeeded in rearing any myself, but I have seen birds of this species which had been nest-reared and were being kept caged; they should be fed as recommended for the Shama, but are not worth the trouble of keeping unless to send to the London Zoological Gardens, which have never yet been able to exhibit this well-known bird.

THE SHRIKES.

The Shrikes are a family of insect-eating birds, found everywhere except in South America, and varying much in size and form. Generally speaking, however, they have a strong, hooked bill, a large head, rather a long tail, small feet, and wings of medium length. The larger ones often devour small vertebrate animals such as mice, lizards, and little birds, holding their prey in one foot, or sometimes impaling it on a thorn. Young Shrikes are noticeable for having a plumage marked with dark bars. Many of this family are found in India, but only two can be noticed here.

THE BROWN SHRIKE (*Lanius cristatus*), figured on Plate II (Fig. 1), may be taken as an example of the typical Shrikes or Butcher-Birds, called in Hindustani generally *Latora ;* the brown species is known as *Kher Khetta*, or in Bengali *Kakhati*. This bull-headed, dark-faced bird is found in winter all over the empire. and about Calcutta at any rate its harsh chattering notes are a welcome indication of the speedy advent of the cold weather. The male and female are alike in plumage, but the young are marked with dark bars, and most individuals show some of these, so the markings must take years to disappear. This bird has a steady, level flight, and watches for its food from its perch, keeping much to the same locality during its stay with us. It is fond of cockroaches, and will readily come down to pick these up if thrown out for it. Other birds do not seem to fear it, but I have seen it attack a weakly Sun-bird.

It is suspected of breeding with us at times, and some individuals are known to stay all the year round, but its real summer home is in Tibet, Mongolia, and Siberia Our other typical Shrikes are much finer and showier birds than this species, plumaged in French-grey black, white, and chestnut, but with an unmistakeable family resemblance to their sombre relative. They all have similar habits, solitary and sedentary, with harsh voices and a deadly grip of bill. They are most useful birds in either field or garden, and should be rigidly protected for their services in destroying grass-hoppers, mice, &c. Those that breed with us make large open nests in trees or bushes, and lay greenish-white eggs with brown spots.

THE SHORT-BILLED MINIVET (*Pericrocotus brevirostris*), figured on Plate IV (Fig. 1) is a type of a quite different style of Shrike. The Minivets, often called *Rajah Lal*, are birds of a harmless disposition only preying on insects; their bills and feet are weak, their wings rather long, and their tails decidedly so, with the centre pairs of feathers much the longest. They go about in parties, fluttering from bough to bough, and clinging to the twigs in search of insects. In most species the sexes are absolutely different in colour, though both are very pretty, the males being red-and-black and the females yellow-and-grey. The young are like the hens, but barred like other young Shrikes.

The Short-billed Minivet is a very widely-spread and common species, being found all along the Himalayas and parts of the plains adjacent to them. It ranges up to 10,000 feet and extends south to Karennee, Arrakan and the Salween River. Eastern male specimens are a deeper and richer red than western ones. The male is the sex represented in the Plate : the hen is yellow where he is red, and also has a yellow throat and forehead; her wings and tail are brown where the male's are black, and her crown and back of a grey-green hue.

With the Minivets it is common to see one red bird with a small flock of yellow ones—no doubt the old pair and their brood; the natives, however, put a different interpretation on it, and call one species the "beloved of seven damsels."

I have seen the Short-billed Minivet in confinement, brought down from the hills in consignments of small birds from thence; but the Minivets did not do very well; being true insect-feeders they need a great deal of care, and I do not recommend anyone to keep them except with a view to export. Such lovely and harmless creatures surely deserve introduction into any country where they could live if turned out at large. The nest of this bird, like those of Minivets generally, is cup-shaped, made of fine twigs coated outside with lichens, and placed rather high up in a tree, the Minivets being thorough tree-haunters, and not coming to the ground as many Shrikes do. The eggs are three to five in number, spotted with red and purple on a whitish ground In the Himalayas the bird breeds in May or June.

The Piping-Crow Shrike or Australian Magpie (*Gymnorhina tibicen*)* is a Shrike of an entirely different type again, of which we have no representatives in India; but as it is frequently imported, it deserves a notice here. This "Magpie" only deserves its name by reason of its pied plumage; in form it rather resembles the common House-Crow, which it equals in size. Its tail, however, is a little shorter than the Crow's and as different as possible from a real Magpie's lengthened appendage. The bill of the Piping-Crow is stout at the root, but rapidly tapers to the hooked tip, which is dark; the rest of the bill is of a peculiar bluish white, with no bristles at the root as in a true Crow. Except for this peculiar beak, which much resembles that of the Australian Butcher-birds—birds which anyone could at once see to be Shrikes—the Piping-Crow is much more Crow than Shrike to look at, having a Crow's long legs and power of running actively about on the ground. The markings of the plumage are very peculiar, and unlike those of any other bird. The head, feet, all the under-parts and the flanks, are black; so also are the wings, but they bear a white patch; the tail is white with a black tip, and there is a white patch covering the back of the neck. The space between neck and tail may be either black, white, or grey, the black-backed birds coming from one part of Australia, and the light-backed from another; but it is doubtful whether they are really distinct species, and for all practical purposes they may be reckoned as one. Male and female are alike, but young birds are thickly mottled with drab underneath, and in buying a bird which it is intended to teach and make a pet of, this drab mottling as a sign of youth, must be looked out for. An old bird, however, will be found to have a most beautiful whistle of its own, rich and varied, which alone makes the species worth keeping, to say nothing of its being a handsome bird and possessed of much character. A young bird which has been properly

PLATE III.

One-half Natural Size.

1.—YELLOW-BREASTED HONEYSUCKER (Purple and crimson, yellow below). 2.—SHAMA (Black, chestnut and white). 3.—PEKO (Slaty brown, white cheeks and black throat). 4.—NIGHTINGALE (Brown, paler below).

taught is a splendid mimic and talker. Being naturally a whistler, it readily learns tunes; and when it speaks, its pronunciation is very clear. Moreover, a Piping-Crow is a *free* talker when it knows anything, which, as everybody has experienced, is by no means the usual thing with talking birds. The bird is easy to keep, as, like a true Crow, it will eat anything; it has the Shrike's habit of holding a large morsel in one foot to tear it. A portion of its food should always consist of small animals or tender raw meat; mice, sparrows or the necks of fowls will be suitable. It is obvious that such a bird is not a suitable tenant for any ordinary aviary, as it is not a safe companion for any bird weaker than itself. On the other hand, it is too big and too dirty for a cage. The best plan, therefore, is either to give the bird a little aviary to itself in the compound, about six feet square; or, after it has got used to its cage or to a little roosting-house which could be made for it, to clip the flight-feathers of one wing and let it roam about by day, shutting it in safely at night.

In this way the bird will be an ornament to the garden, and useful in destroying insect pests, while it is likely to keep in better health when allowed this modified liberty. The Piping-Crow is very popular in Australia both wild and as a pet, and a good many are exported. I have said so much about it because it is one of the best of all pet birds, and practically certain to please anyone who tries it, even an old untrained bird being, as I said above, a very nice pet. Although rather expensive to buy—costing at least ten rupees—the fact that it is a very hardy and long-lived bird makes a Piping-Crow a very safe speculation for any bird-lover.

THE ORIOLES.

These constitute a small family of birds found chiefly in warm regions in the Old World. They are of about the size of a House-Mynah, and usually yellow and black in plumage, with rather long wings, medium tails, longish, stout bills, and decidedly short legs. The Black-headed Oriole, figured on Plate II (Fig. 2), will give a good idea of them, as they have a great family resemblance. They live in trees, feeding on fruit and insects, and building beautiful hammock-like nests in a fork of a branch; the eggs are white with black spots. Male and female are alike in plumage or nearly so; but the young are streaked, and the young hen does not come into full colour so soon as the cock. They are not songsters, but have most beautiful flute-like calls. They go alone or in pairs and are called *pilak* in Hindustani.

It should be mentioned here that the so-called Orioles of America belong to a different family altogether, the Troupials; it is remarkable, however, that some of them display the same black and yellow colours, and almost the same patterns, as the true Orioles, whence, no doubt, the confusion. In form and habits the Troupials are intermediate between the Starlings and the Weaver-Finches, and practically every gradation between these very different birds can be found in the family. A common Brazilian

Troupial (*Icterus vulgaris*), in colour much resembling the Black-headed Oriole figured, but with a Starling-like bill and longer tail and legs, has been occasionally brought to India, and makes a much nicer pet than any true Oriole. For, charming as they are at large, the Orioles make very poor cage birds, and are not interesting even in an aviary. It will be enough to mention our two commonest species here.

THE BLACK-HEADED ORIOLE (*Oriolus Melanocephalus*).—This is perhaps the commoner of the two species I am dealing with, being found nearly all over India, besides Ceylon and Burma, though it does not go far up the hills. The yellow of its plumage is particularly rich and deep, but the female is not quite so bright as the male. The young have the black head streaked with yellow, and the yellow of the body, which is pale, plentifully streaked with black. Their bills also are black, while that of the old bird is a lovely rose-pink. This seems a particularly hard bird to keep in confinement; common as it is about Calcutta, I have very seldom known it to be successfully caged, even though nestlings are often brought in.

THE INDIAN GOLDEN ORIOLE OR MANGO-BIRD (*Oriolus kundoo*) called *Pashnool* in Kashmir, is found higher up the Himalayas than the last species, and is spread all over India, but does not extend to the eastwards nor to Ceylon. It is an even more lovely bird than the last, being all yellow on the head as well as the breast and back, except for a black streak on each side of the face. The yellow is also of a lighter but more delicate shade. The hen has a green tinge on the back. The young in this species are of a yellowish green above, and white with black streaks below, absolutely unlike the parents. As in the last species, they have dark bills, while the old ones have rosy ones.

This species is partially migratory, visiting Turkestan in summer. But the only regularly migratory Oriole is the Golden Oriole of Europe (*Oriolus galbula*), which occasionally but rarely visits us in Sind in winter. This species is almost exactly like our Indian bird above described, chiefly differing by its longer wings and showing less black on the face and tail. And people who admire, as so many do, the beautiful Mango-bird, should bear in mind that its equally lovely European relative would undoubtedly settle in England if allowed, as it is constantly visiting that country, usually getting shot before it has time to breed; and therefore do all they can, when at home on leave, to protect rare birds.

THE STARLINGS OR MYNAHS.

The Mynahs form a very interesting family of Eastern birds, of which the only common European representative is the Starling (*Sturnus vulgaris*) known to the natives in India, which it visits in winter, as the Spotted Mynah. India abounds in birds of this group, most of them residents, and several very common. Birds of this family are very easily recognized by their short tails, strong, coarse feet, and the peculiar way in which the mouth turns down at the corners, as well shown in the Pied Mynah on Plate II (Fig. 4), which is a very typical example. The bill is often very straight, and the legs rather long, the birds usually running instead of hopping when on the ground, where they find most of their food. But they are also active on trees, and strong fliers, the flight being level and steady, with none of the undulating action so common among the smaller species of birds. Not that Mynahs are very small; their size always exceeds that of a Sparrow. Male and female are alike, but the young may differ greatly. Mynahs feed mostly on insects, but will eat fruit and even seed also; they build in holes for the most part, and their eggs are generally plain unspotted blue. They much affect the neighbourhood of man, and are usually harmless, not to say useful birds, besides being handsome and interesting to watch. Their natural song is not pleasant, but when brought up from the nest they show great talent for mimicry. They are sociable in a wild state and not quarrelsome with other birds in an aviary, though they can hold their own, even with larger species. They are particularly easy to feed and will thrive well for a long time. In Bengal they are called *Salik.*

THE HOUSE-MYNAH OR COMMON MYNAH (*Acridotheres tristis*) is found all over India, ascending the hills to a considerable height, as it has of late years become common at Darjeeling. It is a very domesticated bird, building a great untidy nest of rags, straw, &c., in any hole it can find about a house, and walking about the verandah with a view to picking up any remnants of boiled rice, &c., that may be handy. At the same time, the Mynah is not offensively familiar like the Crow and Sparrow, and it is perhaps for this reason that he is so generally popular. Besides, he is a nice bird to look at. His brown plumage, set off by a black head and a white band on the wings and a white tip to the tail, looks very neat and his yellow face, bill, and feet, relieve the whole from dinginess. The name '*Tristis*' or "dull," was given to him by Linnæus, who thought he was a shabby kind of Bird-of-paradise. Young birds may be distinguished by having the head very dull-black instead of glossy-jet, and the bare skin of the face dull-white instead of bright-yellow. This is a large bird for a Mynah, being about ten inches long with stout legs and large feet, but a decidedly short bill. It has much courage and will attack and rout a Crow fearlessly. The cocks also fight fiercely in the nesting-season, rolling about on the ground locked in each other's claws, while the hens look on as seconds. The Mynah, like all Starlings, is very ludicrous in his behaviour when singing, erecting his head plumage and bowing at intervals in a clownish way, which strongly contrasts with his very self-possessed manner on ordinary occasions.

His natural notes are rather a mixture of music and mere noise, but in captivity a nest-reared bird often becomes a really good talker. My friend, Mr. F. Groser, of Alipore, has one now, which speaks better than most parrots, and far more readily.

A hand-reared Mynah may be safely allowed full liberty so that if a talker be wanted it is as well to get several young birds, and cage them separately, when the best can be selected, and the others let out or given away, if they show no signs of a budding talent for acquiring language.

Albinism is not very uncommon in this Mynah ; I have seen two white ones with pink eyes, and two others with eyes of the normal colour (a speckled grey), which afterwards reverted, one completely, and the other partially, to the natural colour ; this being likely to happen when the eyes of a white bird are not pink.

The House-Mynah has been introduced into several other countries—Mauritius, the Andamans, the Sandwich Islands, Australia, and New Zealand. Only in the Sandwich Islands has he proved an undesirable colonist, as he there attacks the eggs and young of the native birds, many of which are only found in these islands.

THE BANK MYNAH (*Acridotheres ginginianus*), is called *Ganga maina* in Hindutsani, and *Gang salik* in Bengali, is smaller and slighter than the House-Mynah ; it has the same pattern of colour, but the tints differ. The head is black as in the other species, but the body-colour is iron-grey and the light bands on the wings and tail cinnamon; the bare face is bright red, and the feet and bill orange, instead of yellow. The young birds are sometimes merely dull editions of the adult, as in the Common Mynah, but more often differ strikingly by having drab heads.

The Bank Mynah derives its name from its curious nesting-habits ; it burrows into banks to make its nests, a number of birds associating to form a colony. It is a curious fact that the bird is particularly partial to the cast sloughs of snakes as a lining to the nest. This Mynah is peculiar to India, and to the northern part of it; it does not extend to the east of the Bay of Bengal, but it ascends the Himalayas to some height. It does not seem to be truly migratory, but the changes frequently occurring in the beds of rivers in India no doubt often cause it to change its quarters in order to obtain a suitable nesting-site. It also breeds in the sides of wells, and I believe in Calcutta affects the Fort Buildings; I have seen it often on the Maidan.

THE JUNGLE MYNAH (*Aethiopsar fuscus*), distinguished as *Pahari* or *Jhonti maina* in Hindustani and *Jhont salik* in Bengali, is somewhat intermediate between the last two species. It can, however, be easily distinguished from both by having the face feathered all over, and not showing any bare skin; moreover the feathers stick up in a small ragged crest at the root of the bill, whence the native names, which mean "Crested Mynah." The light markings on wing and tail are white as in the Common Mynah, and the bill and legs are orange; the body colour is grey, but much darker and browner than in the Bank Mynah, so that on the whole this bird resembles the House-Mynah most, of its two relatives. It it found all over our Empire, ascending the hills up to eight thousand feet, but it affects jungle and builds in holes in trees though often associating with the House-Mynah and sometimes seen in towns.

It is a curious fact that the birds of this species, which inhabit Northern India and Burma, have bright yellow eyes, while those from Southern India have pale blue ones. There is, however, some tendency to variation in the colour of the eyes in other Starlings. More than once I have seen the Common Starling in India with whitish eyes instead of brown ones, and I once saw a Bank Mynah with yellow eyes in a cage with several of the ordinary red-eyed ones. If such a variation proved strongly hereditary, it would of course spread in time over a whole district. It would be very interesting to know if the differently-coloured eye in such cases is associated with a difference in disposition or constitution, and this could easily be ascertained with species so readily obtained and kept as the Mynahs are.

I used to know a very tame jungle Mynah which flew about the Museum compound at complete liberty, and seldom failed to look me up early in the morning, though I did not usually feed him. This is undoubtedly the best way of keeping the common birds—to allow them full liberty—but they must be expected to disappear in time.

THE PIED MYNAH (*Sturnopastor contra*), commonly known as *Abulka* among the natives, is one of our most charming birds. The figure (Fig. 4), on Plate II, gives an excellent idea of it, but it should be mentioned that the underparts below the breast are a pale grey rather than pure white, looking rather dirty. The base of the bill and the bare skin round the eyes are bright red, the tip of the bill being white. The legs are fleshy-white also. Young birds, besides having the neck streaked with brown, show no red about the face, and have black bills and legs. Curiously enough, they also have the inside of the mouth orange, while in the old ones this is as black as if they had been drinking ink.

This is one of our commonest birds, being found over India generally; in Burma it is replaced by a very closely allied species or variety (*Sturnopastor superciliaris*) differing merely in having white streaks on the forehead and over the eyes. It is more inclined to go in flocks than the House-Mynah, and does not come into streets and the actual precincts of houses, though a very usual inhabitant of our gardens, where it must be of considerable service as it is usually seen industriously hunting the grass. It does not indulge in any set song apparently; but its voice is very sweet and flute-like, and it appears not to have any unpleasant notes whatever—a remarkable peculiarity in any bird, and especially in one of this family.

The Pied Mynah appears to be the most insectivorous of all our Mynahs; it is constantly hunting for prey on the ground, though, when the red-flowered cotton-tree is in bloom it joins other birds in drinking nectar from the blossoms. In captivity it needs more animal food than other species. I believe it can, when nest-reared, be taught to whistle very well—which one would expect from the mellowness of its natural notes.

Unlike other Starlings, it does not build in a hole, but makes a big untidy nest on the bough of a tree, several pairs often building near each other. The birds must possess remarkable courage to be able to afford to rear their broods in public like this, for the nest is obtrusively obvious to every passer-by.

The Pied Mynah in captivity is apt to turn more or less black on the light parts of its plumage. I once saw in a cage one of these birds which was pale drab all over the parts which should have been black, the rest with the beak, &c., remaining normal. In the Indian Museum, too, are two skins of the species, one of which is mostly white, and the other entirely so.

If any one is thinking of introducing Mynahs abroad, I should strongly recommend this species. Its breeding habits would render it easily controlled if it showed a tendency to become too numerous in a new country, while its energy in pursuing insects would make it a most useful bird.

THE BRAHMINY MYNAH (*Temenuchus pagodarum*) is a very pretty bird indeed. It is rather small for a Mynah, being only just over eight inches long, and has a very long silky crest, hanging right down to its shoulders. This crest, with the whole cap is black ; the crest of the upper plumage is clear pale grey, and the lower plumage warm cinnamon. The pinion-quills are black, and the tail is tipped with white.

The bill is bright blue at the root, and yellow at the tip : the legs and feet are also yellow. Young birds have no crest, and their colours are much paler and duller than those of their parents : but their dark caps make them easily distinguishable from our other common small Mynah next to be dealt with.

This species is found all over India and Ceylon, but does not ascend the hills to any height as a rule. It is found in Afghanistan, but it is not certain how far it extends in the other direction to the eastward of India. It is not so common as the other Mynahs, and near Calcutta I have never seen it wild, although I found it numerous enough at Dehra Dun. It bears confinement well, and will learn to imitate various sounds. When singing, it looks very curious, with its long crest standing on end and its white-tipped tail spread out. Like the Pied Mynah, it would be a good bird for acclimitization abroad.

THE GREY-HEADED MYNAH (*Sturnia malabarica*), is, like the last species, commonly called *Pawi*, the crested birds being distinguished in Bengal as the *Monghyr Pawi*. It is the smallest of our common Mynahs, being only eight inches long, and slenderly formed, with a longer tail than Mynahs usually have. In colour, it is grey above, the head being a light silver-grey, below it is cinnamon, the tail being tipped with this colour; also the pinion-quills are black. The bill is blue and yellow as in the last species; the eyes white, and the legs dark dirty yellow. Many specimens show a white patch on the forehead and throat, this may occur in both cocks and hens. Young birds are a greyish drab nearly all over, with blue eyes; their small size and plain colour make them easily distinguishable.

This little Mynah is found all over India, including the hills at low elevations. It is not found in Ceylon, nor in the Andamans and Nicobars: its place in these later islands being taken by two beautiful species peculiar to them.

The Andaman *Pawi* (*Sturnia andamanica*) is frequently to be had in Calcutta. It is a little larger than the common *Pawi* and reminds one of a miniature Sea-gull, being white with a pale grey back and black quills. It makes a nice aviary bird, having a pretty note as well as striking plumage.

The ordinary grey-headed species has nothing particular to recommend it in that capacity, nor is it a particularly interesting bird in a wild state. It spends most of its time in the trees, feeding on fruit, though it will sometimes come down on the ground and run about after insects like other Mynahs. But it cannot pretend to compare with them either in attractiveness or utility.

THE HILL MYNAH (*Eulabes intermedia*) is typical of a group of Mynahs sometimes—as in the *Fauna of British India* volumes—ranked as a distinct family, which keep to the trees altogether and feed entirely on fruit. They do not affect human habitations at all, build in holes in trees, laying spotted eggs, and are not able to walk like the ordinary Mynahs, progressing on the ground only by hops. The well-known species mentioned above is a very heavy, thick-set bird, with short wings and tail, deep short bill and short strong legs and feet. The head has a band of bare skin on each side, irregular in outline and ending in loose flaps at the back. The length of the bird is about a foot; its plumage is black, richly glossed with purple and green, and with a white band on the pinion-quills. The bill is rich orange-red, and the feet and bare skin of the head bright yellow; the eyes are dark.

Young birds have a dead-black plumage, and the bare skin on the head lies close throughout, and does not end in the loose flaps behind.

There is a good deal of difference in adult Hill Mynahs, some having much larger bills and better-developed head-lappets than others.

This bird, so widely celebrated as a talker, and known to the natives as *Pahari Mynah*, is found on the lower slopes of the Himalayas, throughout Burma and the Malay Peninsula, in the south-eastern part of the Central Provinces, and the Andamans and Nicobars. I have only seen it wild in the former islands, where I noticed it had a direct heavy flight; but I only saw one pair. It is a great deal better known as a captive, and the speaking powers of a really good specimen must be heard to be appreciated. At the same time, really perfect talkers seem to be rare; I have only met with few, although accomplished coughers, spitters, &c., are only too common! My friend, the late Mr W. Rutledge, of Calcutta, had a most admirable specimen, whose favourite remark was "Not a drop to save my soul!" uttered with an unctuous fervour which ought to have been worth pounds to a Home for Inebriates. And there was another at the home Zoo one year, on deposit, which frequently enquired, "What are you talking about" in a very peremptory, not to say vulgar, manner. But these appeared to me to be brilliant exceptions, and unless this Mynah learns Hindustani much more easily than English, I do not quite understand the foundation for his reputation. There is, however, a better bird than either of the above at the London Zoo at present.

People who would keep this species as a cage-bird should remember, *first*, to get a young one, which may be easily selected by the signs above given; *secondly*, to give it a big cage; and *thirdly*, after it has got its full plumage and grown its wattles or lappets, not to give it much rich food like bread-and-milk and *satoo*, but to feed it mostly on fruit. Fruit-eating birds like these have gross appetites, and too nourishing a diet is likely to give them fits by inducing a plethoric habit of body.

The Hill Mynah thrives also as an aviary bird, and for this purpose old wild caught ones will do quite well, though not suitable as cage-pets. They breed from March to May, which will indicate the time when young birds may be looked for in the bird markets.

CHAPTER IV.

Passerine Birds—*continued.*

Flycatchers, Thrushes, &c.

THE FLYCATCHERS.

These are a numerous body of little birds, usually less than a sparrow in size, and distinguished by short weak feet and thin flattened bills with a bristly moustache at the base. They are generally solitary and have a habit of repeatedly darting out at insects and returning to the same perch. Many species are found in India, either constantly or as winter visitors, but they are not interesting as a group, though no doubt useful in a humble way, as they feed almost entirely on flying insects, with which India is undoubtedly overstocked. Three of the most common and striking species may be noticed here.

The Paradise Flycatcher (*Terpsiphone paradisi*), figured on Plate I (Fig. 2), is well known to the natives as the *Doodhraj* or *Shah Bulbul.* It is, although light and slender in make, a large bird for one of this family, the male being about nine inches long without the long centre tail-feathers, which extend a foot or more beyond the rest. The hens and the young males during their first year, have not this remarkable elongation of the tail, but they are easily distinguished from all our other small birds notwithstanding. The colour is a rich chestnut, the crested head being glossy blue-black, the breast grey and the belly white. The bill is of a beautiful blue, and the inside of the mouth a bright yellow, as if it had been painted with mustard; the eyelids are also blue. Nestling birds have very dull or even brown heads. In his second autumn, the young cock gets a pair of long centre tail-feathers, but these are chestnut like the rest of his upper plumage. In two more years nearly all the plumage except the head becomes white. All red tinge being lost, and he then resembles the figure, and is one of the most beautiful and striking birds in any country. Europeans as well as natives notice him, and have also bestowed on him special names, such as "Indian Bird-of-Paradise," and "Rocket Bird."

The bird is found all over India and Ceylon, ascending the hills to nine thousand feet in summer; in Burma it is replaced by a very similar species (*Terpsiphone affinis*) which hardly differs except in having no crest, the head-plumage being short.

The Indian species, at all events, is not a very abundant bird; I have only seen two specimens in the wild state and these, being without the long tail-feathers, were either hens or quite young cocks.

Mr. F. Groser, who has had much better opportunities of studying it than I have, tells me that it feeds much on butterflies, whose wings it cuts off by the snap of the beak which captures them. Some people say it has a fine song, but the only notes I have heard from captive specimens were harsh and unpleasant to a degree. It can be kept caged, but requires a great deal of care, and ought not to be captured except for purposes of export; it would be a charming bird to acclimatize in warm tropical islands where insectivorous birds are wanted.

The breeding-season of the bird is from May to July, and the nest is small and open, built in a branch. Four or five pink eggs with red spots are laid.

There is a rather pretty native legend about this Flycatcher, somewhat to the following effect. Once, so goes the story, it was a Bird of Paradise indeed, snow-white in every feather, and with *all* its twelve tail-feathers in the form of long ribbon-like plumes. But it gave itself such airs that Allah, to punish its presumption, deprived it of its beautiful plumage. On the bird's repentance, however, it was allowed still to carry two of the cherished streamers, though its face was blackened to remind it of its former shame.

THE FANTAIL FLYCATCHER (*Rhipidura albifrontata*) is a bird of somewhat different type and habits. Its bill is rather shorter, and very decidedly bristly at the root; its legs are a little longer than those of Flycatchers generally, and its tail of moderate length, but broad and rounded. It is about seven inches long and slender in form; the plumage is dark grey-brown above and white below. It has a pair of broad white eyebrows on a black head, and the tail is broadly tipped with white, so that, on the whole, it is a strikingly coloured bird. The hen is merely a little duller than the cock, but the young are marked with buff on the back.

This bird is found all over the Empire, but does not go very far up the Himalayas. It is a most charming little creature, not quiet and phlegmatic like most Flycatchers, (which are rather dull little birds) but always on the move, hopping about among the boughs or even on the ground, and constantly opening and closing its tail, and flirting it from side to side, using it, in fact, almost exactly as a lady uses her fan. It has a pretty little tinkling song, repeated at intervals, and is a very dainty little creature altogether.

It breeds from February to August, building a cup-shaped nest in a fork, the foundation being of grass, with an outside coating of cobwebs. Only three eggs are laid, white with drab spots.

Another common species of Fantail Flycatcher (*Rhipidura albicollis*) has similar habits, but is not so pretty, being soot-coloured all over, except for white eyebrows, throat, and tail-tips.

THE VERDITER FLYCATCHER (*Stoparola Melanops*) has nothing remarkable about its form and habits, and is a smaller bird than those I have mentioned, being only six inches long. It is very strikingly coloured, however, the male being of a lovely pale blue all over. The hen is also blue, but of a duller and greener shade; and the young are almost grey, with buff spots.

This bird is found almost all over the Empire, but not in India south of the Nilgiris, nor in Sind, nor in the Andamans and Nicobars. In Ceylon it is replaced by a somewhat similar but much duller species (*Stoparola sordida*). Out of India it extends to China and the Malay Peninsula. It is a migratory bird in a small way, ascending the hills up to nine thousand feet in the breeding season, and coming down to winter in the plains. I found it common about Darjeeling, and noticed it had a pretty song of its own.

It nests from April to July, building in any sort of hole, in which it makes a moss nest. The eggs are four in number, and may be either plain, pinkish-white or speckled with red.

This is one of the very few Flycatchers I have ever seen in captivity; several specimens have been brought down from the hills with consignments of small insectivorous birds. They seem to do well enough on a diet of *satoo* and maggots.

The Verditer Flycatcher must not be confused with another small blue Flycatcher sometimes seen, the Black-naped Flycatcher (*Hypothymis azurea*). This is of a darker and purplish blue, with a black spot at the back of the head.

THE THRUSHES.

The Thrushes form a very large family of birds, for in addition to the fairly large species to which the term Thrush is usually applied, the small Robins, Chats and Redstarts are included in it. All these birds have a strong family resemblance, but their general appearance is hard to describe. They have a neat well-proportioned form, with wings, tail, and legs, all of moderate length as a rule; and their bills are small and slight. The Nightingale on Plate III (Fig. 4) will give a good idea of the appearance of most of them as far as shape goes. Few are so plainly coloured as this bird, however, and some of them are quite gay. The cock may be either exactly like the hen, or more or less different; the young are generally spotted with buff, and look quite unlike their parents. In this the Thrushes differ conspicuously from the Babblers, which fledge off at once into a very similar dress to that worn by the old birds. Otherwise Thrushes and Babblers are much alike in general appearance, though to anyone who has a little experience in observing birds, the coarse bill and feet, loose plumage, and very short wings of the Babblers mark them off from their more aristocratic relatives at first sight. Further observation will show that Thrushes are usually surly and solitary in contradistinction to the jolly sociability of the others; and that they never take hold of things with their foot as Babblers do, but only use their bill in breaking up a large insect. They are mainly insect-eaters, but the large species also devour a considerable amount of fruit. They are good fliers, many of them being migratory, and fairly active on the ground, where the smaller kinds hop, while the larger ones alternately hop and run, unlike most other birds. They perch a great deal in trees, and often build in them, but do not hop about the branches very much, taking their food most commonly on the ground. Their eggs vary a great deal in colour, but are most often spotted.

Thrushes of one kind and another are found all over the world; the Wheatear (*Saxicola œnanthe*), one of the Chats, reaches the Arctic regions, while the remote island of Tristan da Cunha in the Southern Ocean has a species (*Nesocichla eremita*) all to itself.

Among the Thrushes are to be found the finest singers of all birds, such as the Nightingale of Europe and the Shama of India. They are also much admired generally for their neat and trim appearance; though to my mind far less interesting and less animated than the comparatively plebeian Babblers.

None of them are extremely small, but the largest is not bigger than a Jay. This is—

THE HIMALAYAN WHISTLING THRUSH (*Myiophoneus temminckii*) called *Kastura* by the natives. This beautiful bird is over a foot long, and strongly made, though without the coarse appearance of most birds of the size. Its colour is a rich deep violet-blue, the tips of the body-feathers having a curious glazed or varnished appearance; the bill, which is strong, is yellow, and the legs black.

The hen is like the cock, but the young are different, being duller, and without the glossy tippings mentioned above; moreover, their bills are nearly all black. As they are not spotted with buff like most young Thrushes, for this reason this bird is sometimes, as in the *Fauna of British India* volumes, classed with the Babblers; but it does not agree with these in any other point, so that I keep it here with the Thrushes.

The Whistling Thrush is found all through the Indian hills, giving place in Burma to another species which is barely distinguishable, and probably not really distinct (*Myiophoneus eugenii*). The Indian bird ranges in summer up to ten thousand feet, but comes lower down in winter, even to the plains. It frequents the sides of hill-streams, feeding on snails and other small animals. It breeds in the spring, near water, making a large open nest of roots and moss in a crevice in rocks or other similar place, sometimes even under a waterfall. Three to five eggs are laid, pale grey or green, with pink and brown specklings.

It has a very beautiful whistling song, which it begins very early in the morning. The habits of the Burmese race seem to be similar, as might be expected.

This bird may occasionally, though rarely, be obtained in Calcutta, and makes a very nice pet. In an aviary it must only be associated with birds of its own size, as it is somewhat carnivorous in its tastes and very dangerous to small birds. Care should be taken to give it plenty of small creatures as food, such as shrimps, snails, and cockroaches, and it should have ample facilities for bathing. It has a curious trick of frequently expanding its tail. As it does not appear to be a fruit-eater, this would be a good bird to introduce into countries where birds of the Thrush kind are wanting.

In Southern India a species of blue Whistling Thrush, smaller than the present bird, and with a black bill, is found (*Myiophoneus horsfieldi*), and is often called the "Whistling Schoolboy."

THE GREY-WINGED BLACKBIRD (*Merula boulboul*) is also called *Kastura* by the natives, this name being apparently a general one, applied to several species, including the last whose proper relationships have thus been correctly assigned by the natives, often very good observers. It will be at once recognized by its close resemblance to the familiar Blackbird of Europe, but it is larger, being nearly a foot long. The male is black all over, except for a large patch of silver-grey on the wings; his bill is orange-red, and his legs dull orange-brown. The hen is dull dark brown, with a buff patch on the wings, corresponding to the grey one in the male; her bill and legs are duller than his. The young birds are, I believe, brown with buff spots, like young English Blackbirds.

The Grey-winged Blackbird is found all along the Himalayas, and extends to Manipur; it ranges up to eight thousand feet in summer, descending in winter even to the plains. It breeds from April to August, laying four green eggs speckled with brown in a nest placed in a hollow or ledge, and made of moss and leaves, for it does not use mud like the English bird.

It has a fine song, and will live in captivity in the plains, but I have not seen many of these birds caged.

THE ORANGE-HEADED GROUND-THRUSH (*Geocichla citrina*) called *Dama* in Bengal, is about nine inches long, having a tail rather shorter than most Thrushes. It is a strikingly coloured bird, the male being orange-chestnut on the head, neck, and breast, and French grey on the back, wings and tail, with a white belly and a small white patch on the wing. The hen is olive-coloured where the cock is grey, and the orange of her plumage is less rich. The bill is black, and the legs flesh-coloured.

This bird is widely spread over the Empire, breeding in the Himalayas up to six thousand feet, and distributing itself over the plains in winter; in Burma it is more abundant and less inclined to undertake even this small

LATE IV.

One-half Natural Size.

—MINIVET (Scarlet and black). 2.—GREEN BEE-EATER (Green, black streaks on face and throat)
3.—TAILOR-BIRD (Olive green, white below). 4.—IORA (Black and olive green, yellow below)
5.—SIBIA (Chestnut, with black cap and grey wings).

migration. It breeds from April to July, making a big nest of grass, &c., in a bush, and laying three or four greenish-white eggs with reddish spots. It is sometimes caged, and is a splendid singer; and it certainly does well in confinement.

Before leaving the larger Thrushes, it may be mentioned for the benefit of the many admirers of that bird, that the European Song-Thrush (*Turdus musicus*) will live well for years in India, and give its characteristic song at the proper season. Almost all, however, become subject to an excessive overgrowth of the scales of the feet, as do some of the Indian Thrushes. This bird may be safely kept with small Finches, but it would not be wise to trust all Thrushes in such company.

THE DHAYAL (*Copsychus saularis*) is figured on Plate 1 (Fig. 4), and the plumage of the male thus needs no description, being simply black-and-white, whence he is sometimes called the Magpie-Robin. The female is similarly marked, but dark grey instead of black, and the young resemble her, with buff mottling on the breast and wings. The Dhayal is one of the most beautifully proportioned of all small birds, and very graceful in its movements either on the wing, on the ground, or in trees. It is a common garden-bird, almost all over the Empire, but does not range very high up the hills. In Burma and the Andamans it is tamer than in India, and will even come into verandahs. I have never seen it so numerous anywhere as on Ross Island in the Andamans, where every morning the air was full of the sweet song of these birds. About Colombo it is also common. Everywhere, however, the hen is far less often seen than the cock. Whether there are actually fewer females, or whether they escape observation on account of their undoubtedly more retiring habits, I do not know. The Dhayal is not a sociable bird, and even the pair are not usually seen in close company. It is, however, as above implied, not timid, and could probably be made very tame by a little encouragement, such as throwing out cockroaches or crickets for it. It will certainly readily take disabled insects put in its way, and as it builds in any sort of hole, a little box or even an earthen pot, put up in some safe place, would probably be gratefully accepted as house-accommodation. The nest, as is usual in hole-building birds, is rather a rough affair; the eggs are five in number, greenish with rusty spots. The young are not difficult to rear for insectivorous birds, and make nice pets. But the Dhayal is not much caged in India, as his more gifted relative, the Shama, to be noticed next, is easily obtainable. He has, however, been induced to breed in captivity, both in India and in England. The birds which were bred from here by Mr. F. Groser, of Alipore, were a hand-reared hen and a wild-caught cock, and two young were reared and lived to attain their full plumage; they were brother and sister. Mr. Groser told me that on the decease of the old hen the disconsolate widower was so determined not to marry again that he has killed all subsequent wives submitted for his approval? Where the Dhayal is common, it is, I think, best to leave him at liberty; but it is well to remember that he is appreciated in England, and hard to obtain there; and being purely insectivorous, would be a useful bird to acclimatize in parts of the tropics where such birds are needed. The bird has a wide range naturally, extending even into China, whence a good many specimens are sent to Calcutta, being considered better than Indian birds as songsters.

THE SHAMA (*Cittocincla macrura*), being figured on Plate III (Fig. 2), needs no long description; the figure, however, only represents the old male; the female is drab where the male is black, and the chestnut of the belly is not so rich, nor is her tail quite so long. Young birds are brown with buff spots, but have the characteristic black-and-white tail. The Shama is a jungle-bird, and does not come about houses like the Dhayal; but it is a common and widespread species in our Empire, especially frequenting hilly ground, though it does not ascend the hills to any great height. In Tenasserim the hens are often very dark, and thus tend to resemble the cocks. This is a shy bird in the wild state, and feeds entirely on insects; it builds from April to June, making a nest of grass, leaves, &c., in a hole in a tree. The eggs much resemble those of the Dhayal, but are not so numerous, four being the usual clutch. The bird will very readily take advantage of a big bamboo with a hole in it set up in any place near its haunts, and may thus be encouraged, as it well deserves, on account of its beauty, usefulness, and great power of song. I cannot agree with those people who even prefer it to the Nightingale;

but it certainly is a very much better songster than any other European bird, much surpassing the Thrush and Blackbird. In captivity, at all events, it shows great power of mimicry, which is rather a doubtful improvement to its natural strains, as, like most mimicking birds, it has but little discrimination!

The Shama is one of the most popular cage-birds in Calcutta, and bears captivity very well, living for many years if properly attended to. The cages in which these birds are usually kept are, however, too small, and it is a shame to cover them up as is usually done. The bird, if covered, will sing louder, so Mr. E. W. Harper informs us, in reprobating the practice, but the subdued notes are just as pretty; and after all a bird is a living intelligent being, and should be treated as such, and not as a musical box!

The Shama is well adapted to cage-life, as it becomes very tame and seems contented in a small space. Moreover, it is not at all sociable, being so extremely averse to company that it will not even tolerate the society of the other sex of its own species in the same cage! Nevertheless, it has been bred in an aviary in London by a well-known amateur, Mr. R. Phillipps, and no doubt could be much more easily induced to propagate its kind in its own country.

There is in Calcutta a class of men who make a regular business of feeding Shamas. For a small sum paid monthly they will supply a daily allowance of maggots, grasshoppers, and *satoo*-paste to one's bird. But they must be well looked after, for a day's neglect would be disastrous to the poor captives. Where only a single

Shama is kept, it is quite easy to make up the *satoo* one's self, and a few pice to the sweeper ought to produce sufficient insects for the bird's daily requirements, without having recourse to the daily ration of horrible wrigglers. Insects of some sort or other the Shama must have, however; if they run short, small pellets of raw lean meat, previously mixed and washed, should be given. The *satoo* should, of course, be made up with ghee or hard-boiled egg, or both.

The Shama is regularly taken to England, and may be obtained from the larger bird-dealers there; but it is always an expensive bird, and likely to remain so, as such quarrelsome creatures cannot be taken over in numbers, to say nothing of the trouble inseparable from feeding insectivorous birds. Such amateurs, however, as have kept the Shama are enthusiastic in their admiration for it, and, as it will live well at home if kept comfortable in winter, it is always worth while to take a pet bird with one. If the expense of freight and gratuity be objected to, two or three birds can be packed in one cage with compartments, and the sale of the extra specimens should cover all these expenses of their transport. Hen Shamas are always hard to get in England, as they are seldom seen even in the Calcutta bird-market. Such hens as do turn up are, I presume, birds which were got young before their sex could be distinguished; for all the wild-caught old birds brought in are cocks.

Those who are interested in acclimatization should make particular note of the Shama, for a splendid songster, ornamental in appearance, and useful in its feeding habits, with no possibility of undue increase, would be a welcome guest in many countries. For such a purpose, however, special arrangements should, if possible, be made for the procuring of wild-caught birds.

THE COMMON INDIAN ROBIN (*Thamnobia cambaiensis*), though not so universally distributed as the Dhayal, is still a common bird in India Proper, though it does not extend to Burma, or go very high up the hills. In form it much resembles the Dhayal, but is a smaller bird, being less than seven inches long. In colour it is a very glossy black, but the upper part of the head and the back are sandy brown; there is a white patch on the wings, and a chestnut one under the tail. In Southern India and Ceylon the Robins are black above as well as below, and are classed as a distinct species (*Thamnobia fulicata*). The hen is sandy brown all over, darker on the wings and tail, with the characteristic chestnut patch under the latter. The young are somewhat like the hen, but more or less marked with cinnamon, especially in the southern variety or species.

In their general habits, nesting and the colour of their eggs these birds much resemble the Dhayal; like that bird and the Shama, they have the trick of frequently jerking up their tail till it is quite perpendicular. The smaller members of the Thrush family, indeed, always exhibit a great deal of tail-action in some form or another. These Robins are familiar garden-birds, but they are not great songsters, and are seldom, if ever, caged. Beside the showy Dhayal indeed, they seem rather common-place, though nice little birds in their way.

THE PERSIAN NIGHTINGALE (*Daulias golzii*) has only twice been known to occur wild in India, in both instances in Oudh. It is, however, well known as a cage-bird among the natives, under the name of *Bulbul bostha*, and very possibly the two unfortunate specimens who were "recorded" were merely "escapes." The proper range of this species, which differs very slightly in appearance, but more in song, from the famous Nightingale of Europe, is from Turkestan and the Caucasus through Persia, and it is the bird called *Bulbul* in oriental poetry and legend, the lover of the rose. The name Bulbul, however, must have been early transferred to the birds which now bear it, inasmuch as it is the recognized term for them among all natives.

In Yarkand the Barred Warbler (*Sylvia nisoria*) is called Bulbul, it being the finest songster in that district; and it must be remembered that the Persian Bulbul (*Molpastes leucotis*) is a good singer, as also is a Bulbul found in Palestine and there called by that name among the Arabs. This Palestine Bulbul (*Pycnonotus xanthopygus*) is a bird of about the size of the common Bengal Bulbul, dark brown in colour, with a yellow patch under the tail; it may sometimes be seen in captivity in Port Said. Canon Tristrom, who has heard it in its native haunts, considers that it is a very fine melodist indeed, and closely approaches the true Nightingale in the quality of its notes.

To return to the genuine Nightingale; the figure (Fig. 4) on Plate III, which was drawn from a living bird, kindly lent me by Mr. D. Ezra for the purpose, gives a fair idea of its general form and proportions and also of its simple colouring. It is a little over seven inches long and is a slender, delicately made bird with close plumage. The brown of the upper surface is greyer in some specimens and redder in others, the tail being always reddest; the bill and feet are a sort of horny flesh-colour. Altogether the Nightingale is a very hard bird to describe; but the very absence of any special feature—its well-balanced proportions and unrelieved soberness of colour—makes it not difficult to recognize when once seen. And no other bird at all resembling it is commonly caged. The hen is just like the cock; but young birds will probably be found to be spotted with buff, like the young of the European bird.

A considerable number of these birds are brought down yearly from Cabul for sale in Calcutta, where they fetch very high prices, from fifty to four hundred rupees. The hens, of course, are almost valueless, and as the sexes are so difficult to distinguish, it is necessary, when buying a Nightingale, to hear the bird sing one's self, and also to make sure that the bird one sees really *is* the performer; as there is a trick of showing, and selling, the intending purchaser a hen, while a cock is singing behind a curtain! The song of the Persian Nightingale, judging from a very fine bird of Mr. Ezra's which I have heard, is much stronger than that of the European Nightingale, but less sweet in tone. The birds sing well in captivity in the winter and spring months, and will live for years, but need great care. The *satoo* given them must be of the best, and carefully prepared, and insects must always be liberally supplied. I should recommend no one to keep a Nightingale who cannot rely on a sufficient supply of small grasshoppers, white-ants, &c., to keep the bird almost entirely on such food. The European Nightingale has been bred in captivity in England, and I have little doubt that the Persian bird would breed in India, as I have received accounts of hen birds laying eggs when kept alone in cages.

As these birds nest in woods on the ground, using dead leaves, the best way to get them to breed would be to put a tame pair in a large cage about six feet square, well supplied with bushy branches stuck in the ground, which should be partly covered with turf, watered from outside to keep it fresh, and partly with a thick bedding of dead leaves. A very liberal supply of insects should be kept up. Indeed, it would be a good plan to make the sides of the cage of wire gauze of the coarse kind (in fine gauze the birds would catch their claws) and let in a lot of assorted insects every day for the birds to catch naturally. They would not need cleaning in a cage of the size, and the bath, food, &c., could easily be put in by a small door. It would be worth taking a great deal of trouble to domesticate this superb songster, which, after so many centuries, still maintains, with all nations who know it, its reputation as the most melodious of wild living things. For acclimatization abroad I should expect the Persian Nightingale to be a more suitable subject than the European species, as it does not appear to undertake long migrations as these do. I say these, because there are two species of Nightingales in Europe, the Western

(*Daulias luscinia*) of England and Western Europe, and the Eastern Nightingale or Sprosser (*Daulias philomela*), which last more nearly approaches the Persian bird. All, however, are so much alike that they might be taken to belong to the same species; the Western is the smallest and reddest in tint, and the Persian has a noticeably longer tail than the other two. But after seeing much of Nightingales in Kent in my earlier days, I still find it difficult to notice much difference in the Asiatic representative of the dear brown bird, best loved of all.

CHAPTER V.

PASSERINE BIRDS—*concluded.*

FINCHES, SWALLOWS, SUNBIRDS, &c.

THE FINCHES.

THE Finches are the largest family of birds, and outrival the Thrushes in the wideness of their distribution. They are very easily recognizable by their beak, which is always more or less markedly conical in form, being thick and high at the root and tapering very rapidly to the tip. Of course some have longer and thinner bills than others, but there is no mistaking a Finch's bill. The nostrils are set at the very root, where the forehead feathering begins, and the mouth turns down at the corner as in the Starlings.

The use of this stout beak is to crack seed, the Finches being mainly seed-eaters, and always husking their seed before they swallow it. In fact, they eat all food rather slowly, not gulping it like most birds. They readily eat other things as well as seed, such as fruit, buds, leaves, and insects, and should always have some such food allowed them in captivity.

Finches are, as a family, small birds; they are never larger than a Mynah, and some are among the very tiniest of birds. The short-winged Finches of the warmer parts of the Old World, with, for the most part, stouter bills and coarser feet than the more migratory Finches of temperate regions, are usually separated as a distinct family, as in the *Fauna of British India* series, but there seems to be no sufficient justification for this, and I shall here class them all together.

Owing to their vegetable-feeding habits, the Finches are often destructive in a wild state, though many do good service by eating the seeds of weeds. In captivity they are the favourite cage-birds in most countries, though not in India, where insectivorous birds are more favoured. For aviaries they are popular everywhere, as a large and varied collection of them can be so easily obtained and kept.

They are, however, less easily tamed, less graceful in form and interesting in habits than insectivorous and fruit-eating birds. In keeping Finches together they must be associated according to the calibre of their bills rather than the size of their bodies, since the fighting power of the bird depends on the weapon he carries.

Several species will breed in captivity, and such should receive insects and soft food at the breeding season. At other times, soft food is not good for Finches, as they ought to exercise their jaws and gizzard in feeding, and swallowing a lot of soft pasty stuff, which can be readily assimilated makes them too fat.

However, when they are kept with birds which live on such food, the risk must be run; but they do not usually care much for soft food when not feeding young.

Some species of Finches—the Canary, Java Sparrow and sharp-tailed Munia—have been completely domesticated, and produce their young regularly in captivity, so that anyone who feels compunction at caging wild birds can yet secure considerable variety in an aviary without offending his conscience in this matter.

Finches are not much in evidence as garden-birds in India, except the House-Sparrow (*Passer domesticus*) who ought to be banished as much as possible by every bird-lover, as he bullies and drives away nicer birds; I have seen him do this even with the little Honeysuckers.

Many species, however, are sold for aviaries in Calcutta, and elsewhere—so many, that I am not able to deal with them all, and merely give a selection of species which seemed particularly suitable for notice in this work.

To commence with the Eastern or Weaver-Finches, which always reside in warm climates. One of the most familiar in the East is

THE WEAVER-BIRD, called *Baya* by the natives. The older writers confused two species under this title, and not unnaturally, since where they meet, they appear to inter-breed, and thus become confused themselves. The true Baya (*Ploceus baya*) inhabits most of India and Ceylon; the female, and the male in winter, much resemble hen Sparrows, being light brown with dark streaks; they are, however, smaller than a Sparrow, with stronger bills and feet and shorter wings and tail. Moreover, their plumage is more clearly marked and yellower in tone. In the spring the male assumes a very handsome breeding-plumage; his head and breast become a brilliant yellow, with the exception of the throat, which is dull black; the back is also washed with yellow, and he looks a very showy little bird altogether. His bill, which had been brown, now becomes black fading again when the winter plumage is assumed.

In Bengal and Burma, extending east to Java, is found another Weaver-bird which, except for being usually larger, is almost indistinguishable from the true Baya, that is, the hens and winter-plumaged cocks; the cock of this Eastern Baya (*Ploceus atrigula*) never dons such a bright wedding-garment as the typical Indian bird and is thus easily distinguishable at the breeding season. The only yellow he shows is on the crown; his throat is a smoky grey; and the rest of his plumage remains very sparrowy, except that some individuals, no doubt with a strain of the more aristocratic Baya blood, show a few yellow feathers on the breast.

As to their habits, the two birds may be treated together. They are mainly seed-eaters, but probably feed their young on insects. They are always gregarious, even breeding in company, and their nests are the most perfect examples of bird architecture. They are made of grass or palm-fibre, very strongly woven together, and are in shape like a bulb suspended above by a short cord, and ending below in a long tube. The nest is of course begun from above with the cord, and across the lower part of the bulb, inside, runs a partition, which divides the spout from the chamber or pocket in which lie the eggs and young. The excellence of the workmanship is most remarkable, but the end of the spout is always left frayed out and untidy, so as to give less foothold to an enemy. The bird itself enters the nest on the wing, shooting up the spout or tube. These nests cannot very well be concealed, and the birds do not try to hide them. They always build in company, and the nests are hung at the tips of branches or palm-fronds, usually over water. The Eastern species often builds in verandahs, so that the birds' method of working can be watched. Both sexes take their share, working together till the suspension rope and upper portion of the bulb are finished; then they make a perch or cord across the unfinished bulb, which perch will be deepened to form the partition wall of the perfect nest. On this perch, which is strongly made, the hen then sits, and works on the inside, while the cock attends to the exterior. In a colony many nests are found which do not get further than this stage and as captive males in an aviary seem not to be able to complete a nest, it seems probable that such imperfect nests are the result of the efforts of the male portion of the colony while their mates are sitting. Sometimes they will while away the time by lengthening the entrance-spout, for weaving is a pleasure to these birds, and they really enjoy the work. The nests vary in length of spout and of attachment rope, and usually contain some lumps of mud, the use of which has not yet been made out, but the most reasonable theory seems to be that it serves as ballast. The birds return to the same spot year after year, and repair their old nests if they find them. Many, however, are taken away by the natives, who find them very good stuffing for mattresses, as they are very springy, being so well woven and dried. Weavers are very noisy and quarrelsome birds, and make such a noise when a number are together that it is easy to understand the statement that has been made to the effect that the cocks have no song. They do sing, however, but the music they turn out is so excruciating that it is not appreciated as such.

The hen weavers only lay two or three eggs, white in colour. The young are easily reared on *satoo*-paste, and, when full-fledged, will eat the ordinary bird-seeds. Thus treated, they become delightfully tame, will follow one about, and perch on one's head. I once lost two young birds of the Eastern species which I was rearing, they having flown out of the window. They were away all that night and all next day and night. But on the morning following, I was in the street just outside of the compound and saw them flying overhead. I called to them, and they came down close and allowed me to catch them with very little trouble. Birds like this can easily be tamed to live free about a garden, though some will inevitably be lost in the training, as all are not equally clever.

Native bird-trainers perform wonderful feats with trained Bayas, teaching them to fire a cannon, fetch and carry, and so forth. The Eastern Baya, which is the only species living near Calcutta, is only of use for training or keeping as a pet. It is too dull for an aviary bird, though the handsome yellow-breasted Western Baya is very suitable for this purpose. This species is the only one found in the Bombay market, and a good many specimens are brought down to Calcutta from Lucknow, but usually only cocks.

Anyone wishing to keep Weavers should get about a dozen—pairs if possible—and give them plenty of room.

They should not be associated with any birds weaker in the bill than themselves, such as Canaries, as they have a nasty trick of biting the feet of other birds, and are generally spiteful in disposition. But the bright colours of the breeding males, and their very interesting habits, render them well worth keeping with such companions as Java Sparrows, Budgerigars, or Doves. They will breed in captivity, and should have some insect-food at nesting-time.

Two other species of Weavers are common in India, the Bengal Weaver (*Ploceus bengalensis*), easily distinguished by its blue-grey bill, and the Striated Weaver (*Ploceus manyar*) which is heavily streaked with black beneath.

Another species, though so far very rare and little known, needs mention here, as most of the recorded specimens have been met with in captivity. This is the Large-billed Weaver of the Terai (*Ploceus megarhynchus*) which has been confused with the Eastern Baya Weaver in ornithological works. The male of this species in its winter plumage and the female always is much like the ordinary Weavers in the corresponding garb, but noticeably larger, being almost as big as the *Pawi* or small Grey-headed Mynah. It is also of a duller brown and less streaked; but these points .were not considered sufficient to distinguish it by anyone except Mr. Hume, until I found, quite by accident, that the summer-plumaged male was very different from our other species. It is much more yellow, this colour extending all over the undersurface of the body and nearly all over the head, so that practically the only brown parts are the wings and tail.

My friend Mr. E. W. Harper secured a specimen of this fine bird lately, which passed into the possession of a well-known naturalist at home. This was procured in Tiretta Bazar at Calcutta, and some time later a dozen birds of the species turned up there, and were bought for training by a Parsee resident of that city, who took them to England for exhibition. The two birds, on which I was able to re-establish the species which Mr. Hume had first named from two skins, were obtained from the late Mr. Rutledge at Entally, so that in Calcutta one has the best chance of coming across one of the rarest and least known of Indian birds, only the few specimens I have alluded to being known to exist.

A very handsome foreign Weaver is often to be found for sale in the Bombay market, and now and then in Calcutta. This is :—

THE MADAGASCAR WEAVER (*Foudia madagascariensis*)* called the Mauritius Baya by Calcutta dealers; and the Scarlet Bishop by English ones at home. It is a well-known cage-bird, and has been turned loose in several places and allowed to go wild, as in Mauritius; its natural home being of course Madagascar.

It is a little smaller and weaker in bill than the true Baya of India, but otherwise much resembles it in the sparrow-like winter plumage, which is, however, darker. The hens, of course, always retain this dress, but the cock in spring becomes of a splendid scarlet almost all over, but the wings and tail are of a streaky brown, and there is a black stripe along each side of the face. This brilliant little bird makes a fine addition to an aviary, but should be kept with strong companions, as he may show the vicious Weaver temper. The nest is round, not of the remarkable shape of that built by the Indian Baya Weaver.

The Whydah-birds are not found in India, but are confined to Africa, whence some species are regularly exported; they are allied to the Weavers, the males, like cock Weaver-birds, losing their beauty of plumage after breeding. One species can often be had in Bombay.

THE PARADISE WHYDAH (*Steganura paradisea*).* This species is, when "out of colour," about the size of a Canary, and not unlike it in shape, with a rather small bill; its plumage is pale brown with dark streaks, the crown of the head being black with a few broad streaks of a light colour. The hen is always like this, but the cock, when in full summer plumage, is a very different and most remarkable bird. His tail becomes about twice his whole length of body, and droops in a graceful curve, the long feathers being also very broad. The plumage turns to a velvety black, with the exception of the neck, which is chestnut, and of the belly, which is white. Altogether, he has a very distinguished appearance, and it is amusing to see him, when on the ground, arching his big tail to keep it out of the dirt. The Paradise Whydah is a harmless, hardy, and long-lived bird; but, from the size of his tail, he is not suited for a cage, though a great acquisition in an aviary, where he may be induced to breed. If signs of nesting are apparent, insects or soft food should be supplied; at other times the ordinary canary and millet seed, &c., will be sufficient.

Very different from the quarrelsome Weavers are their near relatives, the Munias, thick-billed little Finches of clumsy form, but very sleek and richly-coloured plumage, which is alike in the sexes. They are usually small, but there is one fairly large species; in disposition they are good-natured and very sociable.

THE JAVA SPARROW (*Munia oryzibara*),* although a foreign bird, is well known in India, being called *Ramgora* in Bengal. Its native home is Java, but it has been introduced into many other parts of the world, accidentally or by intention, and has been wild for half a century in Madras. In the eastern islands where it is most common it is extremely destructive to paddy, whence it is sometimes called the rice-bird; but it is not known to do any harm in India. Very many are imported as cage-birds, and usually come in very fine condition, as they bear captivity well. The bird is figured on Plate VI (Fig. 3), but no uncoloured picture can do justice to the exquisite lavender-grey of its plumage, so sleek that the bird looks as if modelled in wax, while its rose-red beak is as delicately shaded as the petal of a flower. The cock and hen are alike as far as plumage goes, but if several are examined there is a good chance of getting a pair if one picks out one specimen with a noticeably big bill and another with a perceptibly smaller one. As they are very cheap, and several pairs will live and breed in the same aviary, it is just as well to buy half-a-dozen at once, if they are wanted for aviary purposes. For cages the sex does not matter, as both are equally pretty

The young, when first fledged, are absolutely unlike their parents, having plain drab plumage and black bills. The bills soon become pink, but the full plumage, especially the black-and-white head, takes some time to develop, and birds in a state of transition may often be seen in the bird-dealers' cages; though I have never seen a *quite* young one in such collections.

Although Java Sparrows look particularly uniform in appearance, they have produced a well-marked variety, which is cultivated in a tame state in China and Japan as Canaries are with us. This is the White Java Sparrow, also a common inmate of the bird-dealers' cages; it is, however, much dearer than the wild grey birds. It is a beautiful creature in its way, looking as if moulded from snow, and retaining the pink beak of the naturally coloured bird. A good many specimens show some of the natural grey colour, chiefly on the back, and such should not, of course, be bought; but it is generally easy to get quite pure white ones. It is not so very difficult to tell the sexes apart in the white tame Javas, as the difference in the bills seems to be more marked than in the wild birds. Of course these white birds will breed readily in captivity; so will the wild grey ones, if they have enough room; and both may be kept together without much fear of inter-mixture if they have mates of their own colour. For nesting they need cocoanut husks or small boxes with holes in them, and a supply of hay, coir, &c. When they have young, some soft food, such as egg and biscuit or *satoo*, should be provided, and it is as well to get them used to this beforehand.

Java Sparrows are not aggressive birds, but they should never be shut up closely with weaker ones, as they are given to foot-biting, especially the white ones, which are more vicious and bigger than the grey birds. With such birds as Weavers and Budgerigars they will do very well. The cock Java has a rather pretty bubbling song, but the notes of the two varieties are not quite the same. Their ordinary voice is. a liquid chirp, very pleasant to hear, and, altogether, if it could be so arranged, they would be very nice substitutes, as town birds, for that scoundrel Philip Sparrow. I found them established as citizens in Zanzibar ten years ago, and tried to start them in Calcutta, but they always flew straight away, when turned out. However, I have seen a few in the Museum compound, so perhaps they linger somewhere.

The Java Sparrow is nearly as big as the common House-Sparrow, but most of the Munias are only about half this size. They are very commonly kept, but it must be confessed they are desperately uninteresting little birds, and I do not advise any one to begin with them, although they are rather pretty and very cheap. One of the commonest, and one particularly suitable for notice here, as it often comes into gardens, is :—

THE NUTMEG-BIRD (*Uroloncha punctulata*), so called by English dealers, who also know it as the Spice-bird ; by natives it is called the *Tilia Munia* or Spotted Munia. This is figured on Plate II, where Fig. 3 will give a general idea of it. Both cock and hen are alike, but the young are absolutely different, being plain light brown throughout.

In this state they are almost exactly like the young of another very common Munia, the Black-headed Nun of English dealers (*Munia atricapilla*), which, when adult, is rich chestnut with a jet-black head and belly. The Spotted Munia is found nearly all over the Empire, but does not go very high up in the Himalayas; I have seen it breeding in the compound of the Forest School at Dehra Dun. Munias do not breed in company like Weavers, and their nests are very different, being large balls of grass, with an opening in one side, placed in a bush. About half-a-dozen small white eggs are laid, and in the case of the present species, at any rate, the whole family, parents and children, use the nest as a dormitory when the latter are fledged. This is the opportunity of the wily native, who, approaching the little snuggery at night, closes its mouth with a cloth and carries off the inmates.

The Nutmeg-bird, like most other Munias, has a most peculiar song; he goes through all the motions of singing, with rather an extra display of energy, but hardly a sound escapes him audibly to us; no doubt, however, his mate hears and appreciates his "top-notes."

The Sharp-tailed Munia (*Uroloncha acuticauda*) much resembles the Nutmeg-bird in size and form, but is slightly smaller with a longer tail. In colour it is dark brown, with the flanks and belly very pale brown, sharply contrasted; all the feathers have pale shafts, which gives the plumage a streaky appearance. The bill is black above and blue-grey below. This bird in its natural state is not common in captivity, but the domesticated variety bred by the Japanese is commonly for sale both in England and at Calcutta.

These tame birds, rather absurdly called Bengalees in England, fall into three varieties. The commonest show the dark-brown plumage of the wild bird more or less pied with white, some being nearly all white, and some only having a few white feathers, while a great many are half-and-half, the marking being always irregular.

Then there is a cinnamon variety, which is more or less pied with white, like the last, but has the coloured parts cinnamon instead of dark brown. Sometimes a cinnamon bird with no pure white is found, but rarely.

Last and rarest, and much the prettiest, are the pure white birds, with flesh-coloured bills and feet. The beaks and feet of the cinnamon birds are also flesh-coloured, as are those of the dark-pied birds if the white greatly predominates.

Of course all these varieties, being cage-bred, will reproduce freely in captivity, and it would be worth while taking a little trouble to get a good strain of pure white ones. A pair will breed even in a cage, and the love-dance and song of the male will be found amusing, for he can succeed in getting out a few notes. Canary and millet will do for them at ordinary times, but when breeding they will need some egg-food. Any hollow receptacle will serve as a place in which they may nest.

Although known to our dealers as the Japan Munia, the Striated Munia is in its original state an Indian bird, inhabiting the lower ranges of the Himalayas, and extending east to Tenasserim, South China, and Sumatra; but it is not common in India.

The other Munias are far less interesting than these domestic ones, and, as I said above, are hardly worth keeping as pets. Besides the Spotted and the Black-headed species mentioned, the Silver-bill (*Uroloncha malabarica*)* is very common; it is a little drab bird, creamy-white below, with a blue bill and a long sharp black tail. There are several less common species which need not be mentioned; they are all easy to keep, like those I have dealt with. Except the domestic species, however, Munias do not breed at all freely in captivity; in this they differ much from a near relative of theirs, which is often imported, and deserves special notice.

THE ZEBRA FINCH (*Tæniopygia castanotis*),* sometimes called the Rockhampton Finch, is a native of Australia, and has become very popular with bird-keepers. It is a very tiny creature, only about four inches long, with a stout bill like the Munias, but smaller feet. The plumage is grey above and white below, and the tail is black, with some large spots of white at the root above. There are two vertical black stripes on the face, and the bill is sealing-wax red, the feet being of a duller red.

The cock can easily be distinguished from the hen; he has an orange patch on each cheek, his breast is crossed by fine black lines, and along his flanks runs a chestnut band with white dots; altogether he is a very fine little fellow. The young are at first like the hen, but with black instead of red bills.

The Zebra Finch is not common in the Calcutta Bazar, but may be obtained at times, and is always worth getting as it is one of the easiest birds to breed in captivity and propagates as freely as a Sparrow. The nest is not built in a hole, but in the branches of a bush ; a small cage with the door removed will be readily accepted as a substitute. The eggs are pure white. Zebra Finches will live well on canary and millet, but need egg-food when breeding. At all times some green food, such as seeding grass, green paddy, lettuce, &c., should be supplied. The cock has a very funny little song, quite unmusical, but strangely metrical ; it is a stanza of four lines, so to speak, the last much the shortest. The ordinary note of these birds, which they utter continuously, irresistibly reminds one of those toys which squeak when they are pinched.

THE AVADAVAT (*Sporæginthus amandava*), the *Lal Munia*, or simply *Lal*, of the natives, is a very familiar representative of the Waxbills, very beautiful tiny Finches with red beaks of only moderate size. They are very sociable and have pretty little voices.

The Avadavat is a very small bird, barely exceeding four inches; in colour the cock is very handsome, being nearly all red with white spots. But this plumage, in which he is figured on Plate I, Fig. 3, is only borne during the breeding season; at other times he resembles the hen, which is always brown above and buff below, with a touch of red above the tail and a few white spots on the wings. Both have red bills and flesh-coloured feet. The young birds are plain brown with black bills.

The Avadavat is one of the birds most commonly caged in India and has been exported to Europe for centuries; indeed, the very name is a corruption of Ahmedabad, the city whence presumably they used to be consigned. The bird, although not frequenting compounds and gardens, is a very common one, being found all over India and Ceylon, and extending east to Singapore and Java. Burmese specimens, and those from Flores and Timor, are considered a distinct species (*Sporæginthus flavidiventris*), because the males have an orange belly instead of a black one, the ordinary cock Avadavat being very dark below. It is very probable that the light-bellied bird is merely a variety, which has become fixed in some localities. This Burmese bird breeds in October and November, but the Indian one in the rains as well, having apparently two broods a year. The nest is a round one, placed near the ground, and the eggs are white. The cock has a clear and pretty, though short, little song.

The Avadavat lives well as a cage or aviary bird, but seldom breeds in confinement. In a cage he should not be crowded up with Munias, which have so much stronger bills, although this is too frequently done. He should have a little egg-food at all times if he will eat it, and plenty of flowering grass, as well as the usual canary and millet. Well treated, these tiny things will live for years. There is only one other Indian Waxbill, the green Avadavat (*Stictospiza formosa*), whose name denotes its colour; one or two foreign species are also imported at times, and all these very small birds may well be kept together.

The more typical Finches, as opposed to the Weavers and Munias, are usually migrants or birds of high elevations in India, and seldom frequent human habitations. In the aviary, moreover, they are not very interesting, but some deserve special notice, and all are readily kept.

THE TREE SPARROW (*Passer montanus*) much resembles the too familiar House-Sparrow, both sexes being like the male of that bird, for in the Tree Sparrow the hen is just as handsome as the cock. The Tree Sparrow is, however, a smaller and slighter bird than "Philip," has a pinky-chocolate cap instead of a grey one, and a black patch on the white of the cheek.

It takes the Common Sparrow's place as a house-bird where the other is not found, but where the House-Sparrow resides he forces his weaker relative to forego the joys of a city existence. I have mentioned the House-Sparrow but to condemn him, but the Tree-Sparrow is a much more respectable character; he is less rowdy, less impertinent, and less prolific, and as he is just as hardy and considerably prettier, may be commended to those people who go about introducing Sparrows—" to make the place look homelike" as a far more suitable subject than Cousin Philip. Most people do not notice the difference between them, but may wonder, where the Tree Sparrow is the citizen, why all they see appear to be cocks. The Tree Sparrow is in full force at Darjeeling, and is found all along the Himalayas, and from Assam south to Tenasserim. In the plains of India it is wanting; but it has a very wide range outside our Empire, from the Faroe Islands to Java. In England it is not common; it builds in holes like the House-Sparrow, and lays similar eggs.

THE CANARY (*Serinus canaria*)* may fairly be called the most popular of all Finches. A native of the Islands whose name he bears, he has been domesticated for three centuries at least, and is a household pet everywhere. The wild bird is a little smaller than an ordinary tame one, and is in colour olive-green with darker streaks; many tame Canaries show this colour, and many also are pied green and yellow, but the pure yellow has now become the common, and even proverbial colour of the bird. Fanciers recognize two shades of this colour; the "yellow" properly speaking being of a bright rich colour, while the light-yellow birds running into white are called "buff." The true yellow is rarely seen in India, almost all the numerous birds imported from China being buffs, though a few are green or pied. Cinnamon is another colour not seen in Chinese Canaries, but many English birds show it. It is a pale brown with darker streaks; and birds may be pied with cinnamon just as some are pied with green. In England, Canaries destined for shows are colour-fed, as it is called; that is to say, during the moult, they are fed largely on egg-food with which a red colouring matter, mainly composed of cayenne pepper, has been liberally mixed. Instead of green food, marigold flowers are given them. On this diet, they moult out in much enhanced plumage, a yellow or buff bird becoming orange, and a cinnamon one brick-red; greens are not colour-fed.

Of course the effect of this feeding is not permanent; at the next moult, unless the tinted rations are again supplied, the bird reverts to its natural colour. But the effect is so striking that colour-feeding is constantly practised, as no bird with a natural complexion has any chance of winning prizes nowadays in most f the breeds.

A good deal of alteration in the form of the Canary has also been effected since it was tamed. The Chinese birds commonly seen in Calcutta have departed little from the wild type in shape and size. But many English birds are twice as big as Chinese specimens; birds with crests formed of radiating feathers are commor ; and in the Scotch and Belgian Canaries, the form is very large and thin, and the common position a craning or stooping one. The song of the Canary is of course its great recommendation as a cage-bird, as it is more melodious than that of most Finches, and better sustained than that of almost any bird; and in Germany, where the song has been specially cultivated, it has been brought to great perfection, by breeding from the best singers and their female relatives.

In England, song is neglected by fanciers, size, colour, &c., being the points attended to; hence the English birds, being so large and fine, have often very loud and unpleasant voices. But it must be remembered that a bird's song which is unpleasantly loud in the confined rooms of an English house, would not be at all out of place in one of our bungalows.

The Chinese birds commonly to be had in India have nice soft voices, as have also the Maltese. As the cock and hen Canary are almost exactly alike, the only way to get a cock bird, if you are not sure of the seller, is simply to insist on hearing a bird sing, and to make sure you get that identical specimen. Most people like a yellow bird best, but the green ones are the strongest, as is usually the case with domestic animals when they retain the wild colour. Green or pied birds are often called mules, but this is a mistake, the true mule Canary being the hybrid offspring of a Canary and some other Finch, usually a Goldfinch. Real mule Canaries are barren, but they are good songsters and very strong and hardy.

The breeding of Canaries is easily managed. They may be kept in pairs in cages, or a cock and two or three hens may be turned into a small aviary; in a large one more than one cock may be placed, but there should always be plenty of hens, for the Canary, although not naturally a polygamous bird, will, if opportunity allows, take to himself more than one wife, and thus a large number of young can be reared. Only small and harmless birds should be put with Canaries in an aviary, as they are not very well able to look after themselves; indeed, in the French slang "serin" (Canary) appears to be synonymous with "muff" in ours. Zebra Finches and Japan Munias would be suitable company for them, and all would breed.

When nesting they should have little open baskets given them to build in, and some moss and cow-hair as building material. The eggs are pale-blue with brown spots, and hatch in a fortnight, this being the usual period with small birds.

When the young are expected, some egg-food should be supplied, a crumbly paste of hard-boiled egg and biscuit, and salad and other green food be always on hand. Egg-food is also good for the birds when moulting.

As there is a steady demand for singing Canaries, they are profitable to breed. The large English birds fetch good prices, up to twenty rupees, whereas a Chinese songster can be got for five or less. I should advise anyone who wishes to go in for breeding Canaries in India to get some fine English birds and cross them with Chinese hens, mating the best of the hens thus bred back to the English stock, though not of course to their own parents. In this way a good strain could be started at small expense.

If crested birds are obtained, two must not be mated together, or the offspring, strangely enough, will have bad crests; instead, a crested bird should be mated to a "crest-bred" one, that is, a plain-headed bird whose mother or father had a crest. It must also be remembered, in dealing with crested birds, that they often cannot see very well on account of the crest. Desirable as bright colour is, also, it will not do to pair "yellows" together, as if these bright specimens are mated, the offspring becomes lamentably scanty in feather. The proper mate for the bright yellow is the paler yellow or "buff," which has a thicker plumage.

Of the English breeds of Canaries the *Norwich* is about the best for general purposes. It is of good colour and large size, with no marked peculiarity of shape. It may be yellow or pied, and plain-headed or crested. The *Border Fancy* is a similar breed, but quite small in size.

The *Lancashire Coppy* is a very large breed, of which the prize specimens are crested.

The *Belgian* is a plain-headed breed, long and slender in shape, with a very long neck and high shoulders, the head being carried low.

PLATE V.

One-half Natural Size.

1.—PURPLE HONEYSUCKER (Purple, orange side tufts). 2.—SPECTACLE-BIRD (Olive-yellow, white eye rings). 3.—WHITE-EARED BULBUL (Drab; black and white head). 4.—PEKIN ROBIN (Olive-green, orange and yellow below). 5.—GOLD-FRONTED GREEN BULBUL (Green; gold forehead, blue and black throat).

The *Scotch Fancy* is somewhat similar, but has a rather different carriage, the head being higher, while the shoulders do not project.

These curiously shaped birds are not to be recommended to beginners.

The *Lizard* is a small ordinary-shaped bird, with dark plumage spotted with pale, or bright yellow and pale, or bright yellow cap. It is exceedingly pretty, but not very common. The pale specimens are called silver, and the bright ones golden.

THE HIMALAYAN SISKIN (*Hypacanthis spinoides*) is about the size of a Canary, but has a shorter tail. The face, tail and wings are marked with black and yellow, the back is dark-brown, and the underparts of the body yellow. The hen is less bright than the cock. The young bird is duller still, and has dark streaks on the yellow of the lower plumage.

This very pretty and lively Finch is found all along the Himalayas and in Manipur. It comes lower down than most Finches, and I have found it in flocks in the station of Darjeeling in March. It breeds late, in July and August, building, like most true Finches, an open nest; this is made of fine grass, hair, and moss in a branch of a tree. Only three eggs are laid, pale green marked with black. In captivity this bird lives well, and a few may usually be seen for sale in the Calcutta Bird Bazaar. I have no doubt that the cock could be successfully paired with the hen Canary, and the mule ought to be a pretty bird and a nice songster. But most mules with the Canary are bred from the bird next to be noticed.

THE EUROPEAN GOLDFINCH (*Fringilla carduelis*)* is of course only known in India as an imported bird; it does not naturally range further East than Persia, where the range of many European birds appears to end. Its general appearance is well shown by Fig. 4 in Plate VI; it is unnecessary to describe its colouring in detail, as its bright red face and yellow-and-black wings easily distinguish it from other Finches. The hen is very like the cock, being merely a little less bright and shorter in the bill; but the two need generally to be seen together for the difference to be appreciated. Young birds, called "grey-pates" by English bird-fanciers, have streaky drab heads with none of the red, white, and black markings which are so striking in their parents.

Goldfinches vary much in appearance, the Russian, Siberian, and Persian birds, being much superior in size, strength of bill, and beauty of colour to Western European specimens.

The Goldfinch is the prettiest and most interesting of all European Finches, and is a great favourite with bird-fanciers wherever it is found. Its song is only moderately good, but its ordinary notes are sweet and cheerful, while it is lively and active in its movements, and much more graceful in form than Finches generally are. In the wild state it feeds on the seeds of the thistle and other composite-flowered plants whenever it can get them, and in captivity it will eat, and indeed needs, an amount of hemp-seed which would seriously upset most birds' internal arrangements.

It will breed in confinement, and has done so even in India, so Mr. R. B. Sanyal tells me; in Europe it is seldom bred, but very commonly crossed with the Canary, the two birds being kept together for some time to accustom them to each other. The Goldfinch will also cross in captivity with several other Finches.

Goldfinches are most easily got in Bombay, but a few may now and then be obtained in Calcutta too. It is a curious fact that they bear the heat of the Indian climate better than many of the native tropical birds; at any rate they do not pant for breath as the latter may often be seen to do. The only other species of Goldfinch known (*Carduelis caniceps*), occurs in India as a denizen of the Himalayas at considerable heights; but it is less regularly obtainable in our markets than the European bird. It is very like this, but less handsome, having no black or white behind the red of the face, and being of a drab colour instead of brown.

It is, however, stated by some to be a better songster. Where this bird meets the European Goldfinch they interbreed and become confused.

THE RED-CRESTED CARDINAL (*Paroaria cucullata*)* of South America is the last Finch I shall notice. This exceedingly pretty and graceful bird, Fig. 1 on Plate VI, is often to be had in Bombay and less commonly in Calcutta. Both male and female have the same bright colouring, and the young only differ in having the head dull orange instead of scarlet. The cock has a stouter and less tapering bill than the hen, but the difference is very slight; the red on the breast also extends further down in him.

Although several of these Cardinals may be seen packed together in one cage, and apparently agreeing very well, it is not advisable to put more than one pair into an aviary as they are hard fighters. Nor should they be associated with small and weak-billed birds such as Waxbills and Canaries as they have been known to devour the brains of such! But this was probably when they were debarred from their natural insect food; for they are more insectivorous than most Finches, and should always have a few insects or a little egg-food daily. Too much soft food should not be given, as they are rather apt to get unduly fat. They have been known to breed in confinement in Europe, making an open nest in a bush. When they are breeding, particular care should be taken to keep up a good supply of insects. Scarcely any Finch is such a desirable aviary bird as this. It is big enough to be striking, easily kept, and hardy and long-lived in either a hot or cold climate, and its notes are not unmusical, though it cannot be called a great songster.

THE SWALLOWS.

The Swallows are an even better-marked family than the Finches, and, like them, are found nearly everywhere. They have small, flat, pointed beaks, wide mouths, very small legs and feet, extremely long wings, and usually a forked tail—indeed their form is so familiar that they hardly need description. They feed entirely on small insects caught on the wing, and seldom perch, selecting a dead bough or telegraph wire when they do settle. On the ground they are very rarely seen, and when there they walk, or rather waddle, instead of hopping like most small birds. Most of their time is spent on the wing, and they drink and even wash while flying.

They have to come down to get material for their nests, which are made of mud, and generally fixed to buildings, the Swallows having very early ratified an alliance with man, who has always regarded these beautiful and useful birds with favour.

In the Swallows the male and female are very nearly alike, and the young, although much duller, can generally be recognized in each species by their resemblance to their parents. Swallows are migratory in regions where there is a hard winter, but in warm countries many resident birds are found, as in India. The House-Sparrow is a great enemy to them, seizing on their nests, and where that bird becomes common the Swallows are not long in disappearing from houses. People who are fond of the Swallows should keep Sparrows rigidly in check, and put up little ledges in suitable places to afford foundations for the Swallows' nests—it is easy to see where they prefer to build. The dirt made by the birds need be no draw-back, as it is easy to fix a board under the nest to catch it. If thus kindly treated, Swallows will frequent the same house for years, and be of great service in destroying mosquitoes and flies.

Swallows are, of course, quite unsuited to captivity, but, as some one of my readers may be public-spirited enough to try to introduce some of these charming and useful birds into the few countries where they are not yet found, it is just as well to mention that they can be kept, even in cages, for several months, though I believe they have rarely been got successfully through the moult in confinement. Their cages must be large, at least two or three feet long, and have but two perches, which should be covered with cloth, as the birds' feet are tender. The food should consist of insects mixed up in a paste of hard-boiled egg and *satoo*, which they can be taught to eat by giving them insects only at first. Swallows generally are called *Ababil* in Hindustani.

Of the rather numerous species found in India, three may be noticed here.

THE HOUSE-SWALLOW (*Hirundo rustica*) is the best known of the whole family, being found all over Europe, and Africa and a large part of Asia; it is very common in England in summer, and in India breeds all along the Himalayas at moderate elevations, coming down to the plains in winter. To distinguish this familiar bird from other Swallows it may be described; the plumage is steel-blue above and cream-coloured below, with the forehead and throat chestnut-red, followed by a blue-black band across the breast; on the tail is a row of white spots, and the outer feathers are very long, especially in the male, forming the proverbial "swallow-tail" fork.

Young birds are very dull in colour, showing but little blue gloss, and with the face a sort of dull buff tint. A few birds in this plumage may turn up in the plains at any time of the year.

This description applies to the House-Swallow in its pure form, but many specimens show traces of a cross with the Eastern House-Swallow (*Hirundo gutturalis*), which inhabits Eastern Asia, migrating south in winter, when it is common in Burma. This bird is smaller than the House-Swallow proper, and has a less forked tail; moreover its colour is rather different, as the red of the throat runs down nearly through the black band of the breast, and the parts below this are pure white instead of cream-colour.

The House-Swallow builds a cup-shaped mud nest, and lines it with feathers; the eggs are white or pale pink with red and purple spots, and four or five in number; its breeding time in the Himalayas is April and May, and it frequents houses and outbuildings as it does at home. The House- and Sand-Martins (*Chelidon urbica* and *Cotile riparia*) are also found in India, but are not common birds.

THE WIRE-TAILED SWALLOW (*Hirundo Smithii*), called *Leishra* in Hindustani, is a non-migratory species inhabiting both India and Africa, but in the Himalayas it is only a summer visitant. It is a little smaller than the House-Swallow, but has the two outer tail feathers very much longer, so as to look like threads or wires; in the male they may exceed the other tail feathers by five inches, thus equalling the length of the body of the bird; in the hen they are not quite so long.

This is a very prettily-coloured Swallow, the upper parts being steel-blue, with white spots in the tail; the crown is chestnut-red, and all the underparts pure white.

Young birds have duller caps and cream-coloured breasts, and their tails are not so long as those of old ones.

This bird breeds at any time of the year, according to locality; the nest is cup-shaped, and the eggs white with red and brown spots; the clutch does not exceed four. The nest is usually placed under an arch, such as a bridge, but also on rocks near water, and I have found it in the verandahs of buildings at Dehra Dun, the only place where I have seen the bird. It has one note so exactly like the "tweet" of the Canary that the resemblance is most misleading, making one think that there is an escaped Canary somewhere about. In Bengal and Assam this Swallow is not common, if it is found at all.

THE STRIATED SWALLOW (*Hirundo erythropygia*), called *Masjid ababil* by the natives, is a well-known species which always resides in the plains of India, but is not found to the eastward, and is rare in Ceylon. It is rather smaller than the House-Swallow, and has the upper parts entirely steel-blue, with the exception of a chestnut patch on the lower part of the back; underneath it is cream-colour, finely streaked with black. In young birds the streaks are not so well marked, but the reddish back at once distinguishes this species from our other common Swallows.

It also builds a very different nest, this being shaped like a bottle with a neck, fastened by its side against a wall or rock. The eggs are pure white, and only three are laid, the breeding season being from April to August. A very similar but rather larger Swallow (*Hirundo nipalensis*) is found all along the Himalayas in summer, coming down to the plains in winter. It often breeds in verandahs; I found it doing so in the Hotel at Kurseong. The nest is like that of its relative of the plains. There are some other species of red-backed striped Swallows in India, but they are rare, and all the group look very much alike.

THE WAGTAILS.

The Wagtails and Pipits form a family of small insect-eating birds of very graceful shape and active habits which live almost entirely on the ground, running about instead of hopping like most small birds. The Pipits are dull streaky-brown birds, not particularly interesting either in appearance or habits, but the Wagtails are much better known on account of their conspicuous appearance, and it is with them alone that I shall deal here. Their tails are long, but even at the tip, not forked or sloped like those of most long-tailed birds, and they are constantly moving them up and down. Their legs are also rather long, and their bills slender, but of moderate length. They are extremely active birds on the ground, but do not perch much. They are good fliers, and when on the wing progress in bounds or curves, alternately closing and opening their wings. Most small birds fly in this way, but it is particularly marked in the Wagtails. Possibly the idea in closing the wings and swinging along in curves is to get an impetus which their light weight would make unattainable otherwise, for no large bird flies like this.

Although a good many collect together in winter, Wagtails cannot be called really sociable birds, and are evidently happiest alone, except when breeding. The cock and hen do not differ much in appearance, but the young are sometimes very different from them. The nest is made near the ground or even on it, in some hole or other, and the eggs are speckled with brown.

Wagtails are only found in open ground, and are particularly fond of the neighbourhood of water, in which they wade and paddle like Sandpipers. They are most useful as well as ornamental birds, and deserve every protection; they would also be useful birds to acclimatise where insectivorous species are needed, as their diet is so exclusively restricted to insects that they can do no harm at all.

Wagtails are found nearly all over the Eastern Hemisphere, usually migrating southwards in winter, but none are inhabitants of Australia or New Zealand, and one or two kinds only invade America. Wherever they occur they are common and familiar birds, and generally popular. They are seldom kept in confinement, and are not suited for cage-life, but in an aviary they do very well, being easier to keep than most small insectivorous birds. Delicate and fragile as they look, however, they are most savage birds, and it is impossible to keep even two of different species together unless they be cock and hen. In this case, however, they have been known to interbreed in captivity.

There are good many species of Wagtails in India, mostly winter visitors; the natives know them generally as *Dhobrin,* a name which exactly corresponds to the French *Lavandière ;* I suppose the wagging of the bird's tail and its fondness for water have suggested a comparison with the wife of the miscreant who batters clothes.

Wagtails are, as a group, most difficult to identify; it is easy to tell the pied ones from the yellow ones, it is true, but there are several kinds in each section, and, with their changes of plumage according to age and season, they are not the birds for the beginner to attempt to identify.

Fortunately, however, the two best known kinds are easily distinguished from all the rest, and these are the only ones which need be treated at length here.

THE LARGE PIED WAGTAIL (*Motacilla madraspatensis*) is called *Mamula* or *Khanjan* in Hindustani; it is the largest of the Wagtails, and is the only one which is resident in the plains. Apart from its size—it is about nine inches long—its markings are very characteristic. The male is altogether black and white; the general plumage being black, with the eyebrows, belly, sides of the tail, and most of the wing white. The hen is smaller and has the back grey instead of black, but otherwise is just like the cock.

Young birds are drab where the old ones are black, and the white parts of the plumage are not so pure. This species differs from other pied Wagtails in showing so little white about the head. The large Pied Wagtail is confined to India and Ceylon, and is rare in Eastern Bengal, though I have once seen it in Calcutta. It does not go far up the Himalayas, but ascends the South Indian hills up to eight thousand feet.

It builds a small pad of a nest in any convenient hole in a bank or building and lays four brown-spotted eggs. Unlike most Wagtails, it is a good songster, and is sometimes caged on this account, but can very rarely be obtained in the Calcutta market. I do not recommend any one to keep such a bird in a cage, however, as it ought to have a great deal of room to run about and paddle in water.

THE GREY WAGTAIL (*Motacilla melanope*), although more than seven inches long, is a particularly slender and delicate-looking bird, the most dainty and graceful of all the Wagtails. Its tail is particularly long, and hardly ever still. As this bird is usually seen in winter, it is bluish-grey above, except the lower part of the back which is yellowish-green; the centre of the tail is black, and its side feathers mostly white; the eyebrows are white, and so is the throat; the rest of the lower plumage is yellow. Both sexes have this plumage, but in spring the male's throat becomes all black in the centre with a broad white stripe on each side; the hen merely gets a band of black spots on each side of the throat. Young birds are like the old ones in winter, but with a creamy tinge on the white markings of the plumage.

This exquisite little bird is found in summer over most of the northern part of the Old World; in winter it goes south, and is one of the first birds which arrives to tell us of the approach of the cold weather. It is always near water, and has very little fear of men, haunting tanks in gardens. For three years the same bird turned up every winter at the large tank in the Indian Museum grounds, and spent all its time there; I could easily identify it, as by a curious freak of nature, two of the innermost feathers of the wings were white, forming a V-shaped mark on the bird's back when the wings were closed.

The last winter I was in India (1902) I did not see it, but there was another bird of the same kind in the old haunt; large as the tank is, about sixty yards across in the narrowest part, I never saw more than one there.

Many of this species breed at elevations of over six thousand feet in the Himalayas; I have seen it at Kurseong in spring in full wedding-dress. It breeds in May or June, building its nest under a stone or in a bush, of fibres and moss. There are generally five eggs, of a dirty white speckled with yellowish-brown.

In confinement this bird has bred with the English Pied Wagtail, and the hybrids even proved capable of breeding again.

THE LARKS.

Larks are rather small birds of dull drab or sandy plumage, usually with darker streaks; their bills vary in shape in a manner unusual among species of the same family, some being short and thick, and others long and thin; nevertheless there is something about a Lark which makes it easily recognizable. Their wings are large and their tails rather short; the hinder toe usually bears a long straight claw, and the back of the shank is covered with small separate scales like the front. This last point will distinguish the Larks from the Pipits, which also have a brown streaky plumage and a long hind claw, and are often called Titlarks; but they have the back of the shank covered by two long undivided plates, like most Passerine birds.

Larks run about on the ground like Pipits and Wagtails, not hopping like most small birds; but unlike the Pipits, they roll and shuffle in sand instead of washing, and are still less addicted to perching than those birds, remaining almost constantly on the ground. They naturally build on the ground also, collecting a little grass in a hollow, and their eggs are brown-speckled.

The cock and hen are usually alike in Larks, but the young are very different, being spotted with buff like the young of so many Thrushes. Cock Larks are very good songsters in many cases, and are especially noticeable from their habit of rising in the air to sing; some species, however, are much more addicted to this habit than others, and all at times sing when sitting still.

Larks are generally more or less gregarious in winter, and some assemble in very large flocks. They feed both on seeds and insects, and are sometimes destructive to sprouting corn. Most of them are resident, but some migrate long distances, such as the Skylark of Europe (*Alauda arvensis*) which also inhabits the Himalayas. As articles of food Larks have long been esteemed, and the "Ortolan" of India is generally a small kind of Lark (*Calandrella dukhunensis*); but the "Wortlums" of the bird-sellers in the Calcutta Provision Bazaar may be almost anything, and many Pipits and Wagtails are served up under this name. The true Ortolan of Europe (*Emberiza hortulana*) is a rare winter visitor in the North-West, and never by any chance is found in the dealers' baskets! Something ought to be done, by the way, to stop the cruelty of these men in keeping the poor little birds in a famished condition; not even water being supplied them, while they are also very roughly handled, all the quill feathers of one wing being pulled out to prevent their escape.

The natives are very fond of keeping various Larks as cage-birds, and have separate names for the different species; but curiously enough, the Skylark, so popular at home, does not seem a favourite with fanciers in India.

Larks will do well and live long in cages, and will of course thrive well in an aviary also. Not more than a pair of each species should be put in an aviary, as the cocks are very quarrelsome. On account of their omnivorous habits, they are easy to keep; in captivity they take to perching a great deal, if in a small aviary, but not in a large one. They have seldom been bred in confinement. As Larks, although common, are not usually garden birds, and are not very interesting in an aviary as a rule, I shall only notice one species which is particularly desirable.

THE CRESTED LARK (*Galerida cristata*) is well known to the natives under the name of *Chendool*. There is nothing very distinctive about its plumage, which is light brown above and creamy-white below, with darker streaks, most strongly marked on the breast; but it can easily be distinguished from other Larks by its narrow crest of a few long feathers, and by its long thin bill, this being not unlike that of a bird of the Thrush family, but rather longer. The tail is rather short, and the whole length of the bird about seven inches. The hen and cock are alike, but the young are easily distinguishable by their buff spots.

This Lark, although not a very migratory bird, is widely spread all along the Northern Hemisphere of the Old World, and, although it avoids damp regions, has great powers of enduring extremes of climate, and its tastes in the matter of food must be accommodating, as it rather affects barren localities. In India it is mostly confined to the North-West, and a comparatively small proportion of the birds that visit us remain to breed in the country. These nest from March to June, making a small bed of various soft materials under any shelter such as a stone, or even a clod. Not more than three eggs are laid, white with brown and purple spots.

The Crested Lark bears captivity well, and is a very good songster as a cage-bird. In an aviary, judging from one specimen I was able to observe, a bird obtained young, it is lively and interesting, always industriously digging in the ground, and seldom still for long.

It is also very courageous; I saw the above bird once stand up to a Black-throated Thrush (*Merula atrigularis*), a bird twice its own size, and boldly sing in its face till the Thrush gave way. In 1901 I had several sent to England, and let them out in Kent, and I hope they survived to breed. I should advise someone to repeat the experiment, as the bird has already been found in England on a few occasions, and would, if established, probably thrive there. As it is a harmless bird, sings well, and is much more familiar than most of the Larks, it would be an acquisition in any country.

THE SUNBIRDS.

The Sunbirds, commonly called Honey-suckers by Europeans, and *Shakar khora* by natives, are most charming little creatures, only found in the warm parts of the Old World. They are often mistaken for the true Humming-birds, which they resemble in feeding on nectar and small insects, and rival in the beauty of their plumage. But the Humming-birds are confined to the New World, and so none of them are ever to be seen in India. Moreover, they have quite distinct habits from any other birds, being constantly on the wing with a buzzing flight like that of the hawk-moths, which insects they resemble, rather than birds, to an inexperienced eye. The Honey-suckers, on the other hand, hop about the twigs like other little birds, perching on the flower-stems to extract the honey, etc., from the blossoms, and only hovering a little occasionally. They have long slender bills, usually curved, and fairly long legs. Their wings are moderate in size, but although usually very small birds, they fly high and strongly, and do not mind exposing themselves in the open—at any rate this is the case with the two commonest Indian species. They build hanging nests, and lay spotted eggs. The cocks are very brilliantly coloured, but the hens are plain, though dainty and graceful in appearance; the young are like their mothers.

These lovely little birds are very tame and familiar, coming freely into gardens, and allowing themselves to be easily watched; and their nests are often quite accessible. Of course, I do not recommend them to be caged in India, but it is worth mentioning that they can be taken to England, several having been taken home of late years. In captivity they should be fed on honey slightly diluted with water and mixed with *satoo* into a thin pap, with maggots when obtainable. When this is not the case, some crumbled yolk of hard-boiled egg should be mixed up in the pap. There is no trouble in getting them to feed, and they are soon reconciled to captivity.

In any locality in England where some flowers are always in bloom I believe one of our Himalayan species might thrive in the open; this is the Firetailed Red Honey-sucker (*Aethopyga ignicauda*), a very beautiful species which ranges as high as 11,000 feet. But the commonest species in India are birds of a low elevation.

The Purple Honey-sucker (*Arachnechthra asiatica*) is figured on Plate V (Fig. 1); this figure represents the full plumaged male; the hen is olive-coloured above and yellow below. After breeding the cock loses his glossy purple plumage and becomes like the hen, except for a long narrow purple streak running from the chin down to the breast.

This bird is found all over the Empire, but does not ascend the hills above five thousand feet; on the west it goes as far as Persia, and extends eastward to Cochin China, so that altogether it must be one of the most abundant of all the family. It breeds more than once a year, and the nest may be found at almost any time. The said nest is of a somewhat oval shape and hung from the tip of a branch; it has an entrance as the side, usually with a projection or eave over it. The material used is grass, but the outside is coated with cobwebs, and thickly stuck over with dead leaves, scraps of bark, and other rubbish, including even bits of old letters. The whole affair hardly looks like a nest, and, though it is placed low down, no doubt often escapes observation thereby. Only two or three eggs are laid, white speckled with brown.

This is to my mind one of the most charming of all Indian birds. The male, in addition to his beauty, possesses a very pretty song somewhat like that of a Canary, and he is a very free songster, warbling almost continually, even when out of breeding plumage. He is not a sociable bird, and two are seldom seen together. In the breeding season the flame-coloured tufts which spring from the arm-pits are freely displayed, but ordinarily they are not noticeable, though I have noticed that in captive birds they show up when the owner settles down to roost. The male at all events has a strong attachment to localities; I remember one which continually haunted the same two or three trees, and habitually sang from one particular twig. I noticed a similar attachment to one perch in a bird I had caged, which I took home with me in 1900 to the London Zoological Gardens, this being the first sunbird to reach England alive. But as he was in moult when I got him, and the completion of the process was stopped by the journey, he unfortunately did not live long after arrival

The year before I left India, I remember being delighted by an instance of the tameness of these little birds. I saw one on a tree close to my verandah, and wishing to get a better look at him, approached the edge when to my astonishment, the bird began to come nearer, and gave me as good a view as I could have wished, seeming quite as much interested in me as I was in him.

THE YELLOW-BREASTED OR AMETHYST-RUMPED HONEY-SUCKER (*Arachnechthra zeylonica*) resembles the previous bird in nesting-habits and the colour of the eggs, and is of about the same size, but has a smaller bill and very different plumage—that is in the case of the cock, the hens of the two species being much alike in colour. The cock of this species has a dark-red back and purple head and rump, the latter being especially brilliant; the belly is a beautiful yellow below the purple throat. But curiously enough these rich colours are only visible when the bird is close at hand; at a comparatively small distance it appears simply black and white, and this is fairly represented by Fig. 1 of Plate III. The hen is like that of the last species, but has the throat white, instead of being all yellow below; besides which her rather smaller bill distinguishes her.

The male in this species undergoes no seasonal change of colour, but when he has once donned his ruby and amethyst plumage wears it all the year round.

This bird is confined to India and Ceylon, and even there has a more restricted range than the purple species. But it is nevertheless a very common bird and in Calcutta is very much more numerous than the other. It is more sociable than this, and commonly goes about in pairs. It is also a livelier bird, continually flicking up its wings, and uttering a pretty little note like "chi-chit, chit-te-wee;" but the male does not seem to be so good a songster. This species has been successfully kept in captivity. Mr. E. W. Harper sent a pair to the London Zoological Gardens, and Mr. F. Groser had two lovely full-plumaged cock birds as perfect as wild ones, which he had successfully reared from the nest, feeding them at first on small grasshoppers. But, as I said above, I do not recommend these birds as pets, and should rather advise my readers to try and improve acquaintance with them by growing such plants as bear flowers of which they especially approve, or even hanging out little vessels of syrup for them. One of the grudges I bear against Philip Sparrow is that I have seen him drive away these harmless little things when a pair actually came to my verandah, the hen picking up bits of fluff for nesting material; in the absence of this feathered hooligan I have no doubt we should see far more of the numerous more attractive small birds.

THE FLOWER-PECKERS.

These tiny creatures, the smallest birds of the Old World, to the warm parts of which they are confined, are little known, though not rare. As they are so very tiny, smaller even than Waxbills or White-eyes, and keep to the tops of high trees, where they feed on berries, insects, etc., it is not easy to make their acquaintance. Fortunately, however, it is sometimes possible to obtain specimens of them alive, and they can be kept in captivity. They always have rather short tails, but their bills may be either thick or thin and, when looked at under a hand-lens are found to be saw-edged, as are also those of the Honey-suckers.

THE SCARLET-BACKED FLOWER-PECKER (*Dicæum cruentatum*) is represented in Fig. 5 of Plate I. Although barely larger than a big bee, the male—which is the sex figured—is a very showy little thing, with his cream-coloured breast and glossy black upper plumage decorated by a broad splash of scarlet from crown to tail. The hen is olive-green with a black tail, and a dash of scarlet on the back just at the root of it. The young are like her. The exact range of this minute bird is not known, but it is not uncommon in the eastern parts of India, and in Burma, whence it spreads even to South China and Sumatra. It is common about Calcutta, but I never saw it wild there. It breeds from March onwards, building a little oval nest of grass and the down of plants, which is hung from the tip of a high branch; the two or three eggs it contains are pure white.

Occasionally this bird might have been obtained from the late Mr. W. Rutledge, the only dealer I have known to have it. When several are in an ordinary cage together, they seem to be peaceable enough, but I found on buying two cocks and a hen and turning them out into a large verandah cage, that the cocks fought like fiends, and soon both were dead. They appeared not to care for the company of other little birds, but were not aggressive to them. Mr. E. W. Harper succeeded in sending this species to the London Zoological Gardens, and also the still tinier Tickell's Flower-pecker (*Dicæum erythrorhynchum*) a plain drab bird with a flesh-coloured bill; the latter was the first bird of this family to reach England alive. A large cage is more suitable for birds like these than an aviary: they should be fed on soft food and a paste of hard-boiled yolk of eggs mixed up with honey and *satoo* or biscuit-crumbs. The Crimson-backed Flower-pecker is a remarkably greedy feeder for its size, like most small birds. The most charming thing about them is their extreme fearlessness of man; they will come on to one's hand without hesitation when hungry, and altogether are delightful little pets, which I strongly recommend to anyone who can only keep such birds as will live in a cage small enough to be carried about. Of course care must be taken to shield them from cold; if this be done they can be taken to England, and will always be welcome to fanciers there. I am glad to say that the bird sent by Mr. Harper to the London Zoo lived for some time there.

THE PITTAS.

Few families of birds are more suited to be aviary pets than these, although as yet they are little known in that capacity. They are found, though not abundant birds, all through the warm parts of the Old World, usually keeping to jungle though coming into gardens. In size they are about equal to the smaller Mynahs, but in form and action more resemble the Thrushes, with which they used to be classed. Their bills are rather stouter than an ordinary Thrush's, and their legs longer, while their tails are absurdly short and hardly noticeable.

They live mostly on the ground, and do not perch much; but unlike most ground birds, they never run, but always hop, though they get along in this manner very swiftly and gracefully. They are fairly good flyers, but usually keep low down. They seem to feed entirely on insects and other small animals, and they are not at all sociable, being usually seen alone. They do not sing, but their plumage is usually remarkably brilliant and beautiful, and shows a great variety of patterns. Their nests are domed and placed either on the ground or near it, and they lay spotted eggs.

THE BENGAL PITTA (*Pitta brachyura*). This species, known to the natives as *Nowrung* or "nine colours," is the most familiar of all, being found all over India and Ceylon in the plains. It is to a certain extent migratory, going south in the winter, and returning to the northern provinces in the hot weather and rains, though some birds appear never to change their quarters.

In colour it is green above and buff below, with the head broadly streaked with black and drab, the throat white, and a patch under the tail scarlet. On the shoulder of the wing, and just above the root of the very short tail, are patches of intense shining sky-blue, and the flight feathers of the wings are black with a large white patch, as in the House-Mynah. The bill is salmon-coloured and black, and the legs flesh-coloured, the eyes being dark brown. The cock and hen are alike, and the young closely resemble them, being merely duller in colour below, where there is also a slight dark edging to the feathers. Some of the skins of this species in the Indian Museum have the back marked with black streaks in the centre of the feathers, both the green and blue portions; one specimen is very perfectly streaked on every feather, and from this there is a gradation to that of ordinary birds. But I have never seen any of the living birds brought in for sale marked in this way, and as the books say nothing about it, it must be rather a rare variation.

This bird breeds, in the Central Provinces at least, in July and August, and builds a big round nest of twigs and leaves. This is either actually on the ground or on a low branch. The eggs are lustrous white with deep red and purple spots. The young are sometimes reared from the nest and brought to Calcutta for sale, but only occasionally.

They get very tame and make most charming pet birds, but are not suited for cage life in some ways, as besides not being songsters, they scatter the sand about so much by their active movements that the vicinity of the cage is always dirty. If, therefore, they have to be kept caged, a hay bedding is better than a sanded floor. It is in an aviary or very large cage, however, that they really do themselves justice. Their ordinary movements are very graceful, and their gestures when excited are most amusing. Sometimes they will stand bolt upright, at others crouch down; and in either position they will often expand their wings, an action which has a most ludicrously oratorical appearance when they are standing up. With other birds they seem to be quite harmless, even with much smaller ones, but they are liable to fight savagely amongst themselves, so that it must not be expected that more than a pair will live together permanently; and there is some risk even in putting cock and hen together. Pittas have never been bred in captivity, so that some interesting discoveries very likely await any one who will devote himself to the study of their breeding habits.

They are not difficult to feed; ghee-and-*satoo* paste, with a little finely-minced raw meat worked up in it, will do very well as a staple food, and if plenty of maggots are available the meat may be omitted. But plenty of cockroaches, grasshoppers, etc., should always be provided, and any fruit which they may show an inclination for should be given.

Pittas have been taken to England alive on a few occasions, but are never likely to become common with amateurs there, and so are always worth taking home. On account of their active habits and compact shape, they are easy to keep in good condition even in a small cage, but they must be kept warm.

CHAPTER VI.

WOODPECKERS, BARBETS, ETC.

THE Pittas bring us to the end of the Passerine birds, and the few species I shall have to deal with now will belong to quite other groups, which are easily made out.

THE WOODPECKERS.

These are known to the natives as *Kat-tokra*, and are very easily recognizable birds. They have a straight, tapering, chisel-tipped bill and feet with only two toes in front and one or two behind; the outer front toe being as it were turned back, so that the real hind toe is rather thrown into the shade, and is often very small, or may be dispensed with altogether.

The tongue of a Woodpecker is a most curious structure; it is long and wormlike, with a horny tip furnished with numerous barbs, and can be shot out of the mouth for some distance, the arms of the hyoid or tongue-bone being long and curved right round over the head under the scalp, and acting like a pair of springs. In young birds the barbs at the tip of the tongue are not developed at first.

Another very characteristic point of the structure of most Woodpeckers is the tail. This is rather short, with very stiff, hard feathers, and is pressed against the bark to act as a prop when the bird is climbing. For Woodpeckers do not usually hop about the twigs like most perching birds, but climb up the trunks and along the branches; they never climb downwards, but if they want to descend let themselves down backwards; they are very quick and clever at moving along sideways and even upside down. Their wings are only moderately long, and they have a very characteristic flight, dipping and rising by alternately fluttering and closing their wings, although they are usually fair-sized birds; but ordinarily they only go from tree to tree. They do not come to the ground much as a rule, and when there move by awkward hops.

The eggs of Woodpeckers are always white and are laid in holes pecked out in trees by the old birds, without any lining. The young are hatched naked and have a curious warty pad on the hock-joint, upon which they shuffle about, not standing up on their toes till they are fledged. Unlike most young birds, they often show their sex as soon as they are fledged, resembling the old birds in the comparatively small differences which distinguish the sexes of these. Woodpeckers are often gaily-coloured birds, but they do not sing, and generally have very harsh notes. They are very striking and ornamental, however, and particularly useful birds, as they feed almost entirely on insects, which they dig out of decaying wood or extract from under bark with their strong bills and long barbed tongues. Thus they keep in check a class of insects which are left alone by other birds, and, although they do not go in flocks, being usually solitary, must do a great deal of good.

They are found almost everywhere, usually as residents, but are absent from Australia, New Zealand and the Pacific region generally; it is to be hoped that some day measures will be taken for introducing them there also, where they would be of the greatest service. They can be kept in confinement, but are not often to be seen in that condition; and one at least of them is a familiar garden bird in many parts of India.

THE GOLDEN-BACKED WOODPECKER (*Brachypternus aurantius*) is about as large in the body as the House-Mynah, but is a longer-shaped bird, measuring about a foot in length. It is very handsomely coloured, the back being of an old-gold hue, while the face, neck, and underparts are marked with black and white, and a flaming scarlet crest adorns the back of the head; the pinion-quills are black with white spots, and the tail all black. The hen only differs from the cock in having the forehead black with white spots; the red on the male's head extends right up to the root of the beak. Most young hens have a plain black forehead, but some have it spotted. Young birds have a yellow tinge on the white portions below. The inner hind toe in this species is a mere rudiment, and not noticeable till looked for.

This Woodpecker is found all over India and Ceylon in the plains, but not in the countries east of Bengal and Cachar, where it is replaced by a very similar species with no hind toe at all (*Tiga javanensis*). It is paler in colour in Sind, and becomes darker in Southern India and Ceylon; a good many specimens show a tinge of red on the yellow back. It is very commonly seen about gardens, and still more often heard, its excruciatingly harsh cackle being given off frequently, and always, apparently, when it takes wing. It is not a very shy bird, and can be easily watched. In Northern India it breeds twice a year, in March and April, and again in June and July; in Ceylon the season is February to June. Young birds of this species may often be found in the Calcutta Market, and are well worth rearing as pets, as they are not difficult to bring up, and become very tame. One I had used to climb all over me, exploring with its tongue, and tapping with its bill on the top of my head. Such a bird could with care be allowed its liberty, as was done with this.

In an aviary, this Woodpecker thrives well, and may be kept even with smaller birds; but it should not be confined too closely with these, or even with its own species. Woodpeckers need good feeding in captivity; *satoo* worked up with minced raw meat or hard-boiled egg, and such insects as can be procured, will do well for them, and they can be easily reared on such food. They will eat plantain readily and should have some of this or any other fruit they care to take. The gold-backed Woodpecker has very seldom been taken to Europe, and so is always worth its carriage home.

THE BARBETS.

The birds of this family resemble Woodpeckers in many points, and are often spoken of as such by Europeans in India, but though they might well be placed in the same "order," they may fairly claim a family difference. The figure (Fig. 1) in Plate I of the Coppersmith will give a good idea of their general form, although most have a rather longer bill and tail than that bird. The beak has a straggly moustache of bristles at the root, and is much stouter than a Woodpecker's; it is not used for pecking into wood, except when the birds are boring a nest-hole. The tongue is of ordinary shape, and the tail is not stiff, but of ordinary feathers. The feet have two toes before and two behind, but the birds do not climb like Woodpeckers, but simply hop from branch to branch, picking the fruit on which they feed, for their diet is almost altogether vegetarian. They hop like Woodpeckers when on the ground, though I never saw a Barbet there in the wild state; their flight also much resembles that of a Woodpecker, and they lay white eggs in a hewn-out nest-hole also. Moreover, the young show the same warty pad on the hocks as young Woodpeckers, and move in the same way. They are often less like the old ones when fledged than young Woodpeckers are, but are quite recognizable. Barbets run to very brilliant and barbaric colouring as a rule and the hens are generally coloured like the cocks. As a lively green is commonly the predominating colour in their costume, they are not easy to see in the trees, but they take good care to be heard pretty constantly. Their notes are not harsh and explosive like those of the Woodpeckers; rather mellow indeed, but of a deadly monotony, being kept up with relentless regularity for a long time.

They begin practising even as nestlings, and are certainly untiring songsters according to their lights. In disposition they are gloomy and unsociable, but not ferocious; that is, they are hard biters, but do not go out of their way for a fight. Barbets are found all round the world in most warm climates, but not in the Australian region. The huge-billed Toucans of America are closely related to the Barbets, but are not found in India, the birds often so called there being Hornbills, which are a distinct family altogether, confined to the Old World.

In confinement Barbets live very well, and are ornamental in an aviary; if reared from the nest they become very tame, and they are easy to manage, as they can be fed on fruit from the first, and so give less trouble than most young birds. They are gross feeders, and eat a great deal of food, so that the more fruit they get, the better, as fruit is not so fattening as *satoo* or sop. They must not as a rule be shut up closely together, as they will fight to the death in such a case, and it is as well not to have more than a pair of each kind even in an aviary.

THE COPPERSMITH OR CRIMSON-BREASTED BARBET (*Xantholaema haematocephala*) called *Tambayat* in Hindustani, and *Chota bussunt* in Bengal, is a very well-known garden bird all over the Empire, but does not go any distance up the hills. Outside our limits it ranges east as far as the Philippines, so that, although it is one of the smallest of our Barbets, it extends over a very wide territory. Common as it is in Calcutta, where one may see it even in the trees lining the streets, it is not very well known by sight, as it is not easy to discover at first; its green plumage blending with the foliage, while the yellow of its face, and the bright red of its forehead, gorget, and feet are not nearly so noticeable as might be expected. Young birds are still less striking in appearance in a tree, as they have no red on the head or breast, and their feet are merely flesh-colour. Light varieties of the Coppersmith are sometimes seen; there was one in the Calcutta Zoological Garden when I left India in 1902 which was yellow splashed with green, and with the usual red markings, but with the bill flesh-coloured instead of black.

What makes the Coppersmith so well-known is his voice, which is a single note exactly resembling the tap of a hammer on metal, and given out very persistently all through the warm months of the year; in the cold weather he is generally silent. I say "he," but both sexes call, and even the young begin, in voices of infantile squeakiness, before they are fledged. In Northern India the Coppersmith breeds from March to June, beginning earlier further south, and continuing in Ceylon all through the first half of the year. The young ones are very pretty little things, easily reared and kept if a satoo-diet be avoided, though bread-and-milk sop suits them well enough; plantains of course should always be supplied, and I have always reared them on these. Old birds can also be got to feed and live in confinement if plantain be given, but there is not much point in keeping these, or indeed any of this common species, unless one is going home. Then it would be worth while to take a few, as Coppersmiths are decided rarities in England.

THE BLUE-THROATED BARBET (*Cyanops asiatica*) called *Burra bussunt* in Bengal, is a much larger bird than the Coppersmith, being about the size of a House-Mynah, but more stoutly built: it has a longer bill and tail than the small Barbet.

It is a very showy bird, being bright green almost all over, with a sky-blue face and throat and a scarlet cap crossed by a black band; at each side of the neck is also a scarlet spot. The bill is pale yellow with a black streak along the ridge. The young birds are more like the old ones than is the case with the Coppersmith, but their head colouring is so dingy that their youth is perceptible at a glance. This Barbet is found on the lower slopes of the Himalayas, and in Bengal, Assam, and Burma. In Calcutta it is common, though less so than the Coppersmith, and, like Barbets generally, much more heard than seen. It has a rolling triple call, like "*kuturuk*" and is as noisy in its way as the Coppersmith, though less noticeable.

It is the easiest Barbet to keep in confinement, as it can be tamed at any age and will live on satoo; moreover, several birds can be placed in the same cage with impunity. Accordingly, the Blue-faced Barbet is often to be found in the dealers' cages in Calcutta, and a good many are sent to England, and turn up not unfrequently at bird-shows. In a mixed aviary of the larger birds this Barbet is always worth keeping where it is not naturally found, and is generally much admired for its fine colours.

THE ROLLERS.

The Rollers form a small family of insectivorous birds of rather large size, found in the warm and temperate regions of the Old World. They are nearly as big as the House-Crow, and have strong crow-like bills, large wings, and tail of moderate length. Their legs are short, scaled behind as well as in front, and the toes are three before and one behind, the hinder toe being the smallest, and the outer front toe as long as the middle one. I go into these details, because the Rollers, being of about the same size and having much blue in their plumage, are often called Jays, especially in India. The Jay's foot, however, is very different from a Roller's both in the scaling and the proportions of the toes, resembling in these points a Crow's as described in Chapter II. The Rollers differ much in their habits from the active and skulking Jays; they sit about most of the time, swooping down occasionally for their food from their conspicuous perch; they do not eat vegetable food and they build in holes, laying white eggs quite unlike those of any of the Crow tribe. As a matter of fact, they are nearly related to the Kingfishers. The cock and hen are always alike, and the young much resemble them.

THE INDIAN ROLLER OR BLUE-JAY (*Coracias indica*), is called *Nilkant* by the natives, and is sacred to Siva. Most people know this magnificent bird by sight. About the size of a pigeon, its slow, lazy flight makes the pale-blue and purple bands of its wings and tail conspicuous; though when it is on the ground or a perch, the drab, sea-green, and dull pink of its body-colour render it a quite unobtrusive object. Our American winter-visitors have neatly expressed the contrast in the flying and sitting Blue-Jay by calling it the "surprise-bird;" but this name would even better fit the Paddy-bird or Pond-Heron (*Ardeola grayi*) which is hard to see at all in repose, and pure white when it flies. This Roller is found almost all over India and Ceylon in the plains, and extends westwards along the Persian Gulf, and even occasionally as far as Asia Minor. It likes open country, and always chooses a perch which gives it a good outlook, very often a telegraph wire, where it remains quite comfortably even in the broiling sun of mid-day. It may sometimes be seen sitting on the ground, or even hopping a few steps, but as a rule it only comes down to pick up something to eat. It is very active on the wing when it likes, in spite of the apparent listlessness of its ordinary flight. Its note is a single croak, varied occasionally by a cackling laugh.

It breeds at various times, according to locality, during the first half of the year, and will often use a hole in a building. Some birds line the nest with grass or rags, etc., but others eschew bedding altogether. The young birds look very pretty when covered with feathers, and can be easily reared on bits of raw meat, cockroaches, etc., but I cannot recommend them as interesting pets, as they are not musical and very sluggish in their habits. If a bird were trained to fly freely about the garden it would be a nice pet, but the Blue-Jay must have room and reason to show its wings if he is to be admired. Old birds can be got to feed in captivity by putting them in a moderate-sized cage and giving them live insects at first; when the birds are taking meat regularly it is as well to mix it up with some satoo or boiled rice to render it less heating. The Roller does well as an aviary bird and is quiet with others, unless they are small enough to swallow, when he is by no means to be trusted—and his swallowing powers are much greater than would appear at first sight. Rollers are very seldom to be had in England, so that a good healthy specimen is always worth taking home. This is another of the birds which ought to be spread by acclimatization, as it is a charming landscape ornament and very useful in destroying large insects.

THE BURMESE ROLLER (*Coracias affinis*). This species is included under the same name of "Blue-Jay" as the last, but it is distinct from the Indian bird, though the difference is not very great, consisting in slightly larger size and decidedly darker colour. The body-colour of the Burmese bird is darker brown than that of its Indian relation, thus showing up the sea-green cap better; but there is no purple band at the tip of the tail, which is all light blue except at the root; the most striking difference, however, is in the lining of the wings, which is pale blue in the Indian Roller, and purple in the present bird.

The young in this species are noticeably different from their parents, being much lighter in colour; the absence of the purple tip to the tail, however, is always characteristic.

This Roller, which has the same habits as the last, is the common one of Burma, and extends east to Siam and Cochin China; it extends westwards into Assam, Cachar, Sylhet and Tipperah, and even as far as Calcutta, but from that place eastwards for a considerable distance the birds are of mixed blood, for the two species interbreed freely, in spite of the theories of those naturalists who maintain that the distinctive markings of closely related birds like this serve the purpose of preventing *mésalliances.* Similar cases are those of the Goldfinches and Swallows, which I have already mentioned, but no acquaintance with such facts hampers the average Zoological theorist!

THE BEE-EATERS.

Bee-eaters are birds of rather small size, with long curved bills and very small feet; there are three toes in front joined together in a common skin, and one behind. The wings are powerful, and the birds live on insects captured in flight. The plumage is always very pretty; the cock and hen are alike in colour, and the young closely resemble them. The Bee-eaters lay white eggs in a burrow which they dig out themselves, many pairs breeding in company.

They are found in warm and temperate climates in the Old World, and several kinds are to be seen in India. Of these one is among the commonest birds in the country.

THE GREEN BEE-EATER (*Merops viridis*). This bird, commonly called a Flycatcher by Europeans and known in Hindustani as *Patringa*, and in Bengali as *Banspati*, is conspicuous everywhere by its beautiful green plumage and habit of sitting motionless on a perch and flying out every now and then after some passing insect.

The figure (Fig. 2) on Plate IV will give a good idea of its form. In colour it varies somewhat; it is found almost all over India, Ceylon, and Burma, though it does not ascend the hills; and specimens from the eastern portions of its range are more or less bronzed on the head, while in the North-West of India the throat is often blue. Out of India it is found as far as North-East Africa on the west, and Cochin China on the east.

It breeds from March till June, making the usual burrow. It is a lively cheerful little bird, with a pretty chirping note and very graceful flight. It is so active on the wing that it may be seen to take its bath by plunging, like a swallow; it is also fond of dusting itself, and several will settle on a road together to indulge in a scuffle among the sand. It could probably be kept in confinement, but is far better left to enjoy its liberty.

THE KINGFISHERS.

Kingfishers are found all over the world, and vary considerably in size; but they are always easily recognizable, having very large heads, with a long straight stout bill; their tongues are, on the other hand, very small, Their feet are small, with three united toes in front, and one behind, as in the Bee-eaters.

Like those birds, they burrow out a nest in a bank and lay white eggs; but they are not in the least sociable and it is only in the breeding-season that one sees even a pair together. Their plumage is usually very showy, the cock and hen being nearly or quite alike; the young also have nearly the same plumage from the first. They are hatched naked, and when fledging are most curious little objects, covered with spine-like pin-feathers, and with a remarkable power of running backwards, which must be useful to them in their underground tunnel at home. A Kingfisher's nest is always in a very filthy state, and there is no bedding except the fish-bones, etc., cast up in quids after the flesh has been digested by the birds.

Young Kingfishers are easily reared on fish, and may be trained to eat raw meat; but these birds cannot be called desirable pets, and are better left at large. The beautiful little Kingfisher of Europe (*Alcedo ispida*) is very common in India, as also is the pretty black-and-white Pied Kingfisher (*Ceryle varia*); but only one of the family can be called a garden-bird. Kingfishers generally are called *Kilkila* in Hindustani, and *Machranga* in Bengali.

THE WHITE-BREASTED KINGFISHER (*Halcyon smyrnensis*) is a very showy bird about as big as a House-Mynah, with a very big head and bill and fairly long tail. Its plumage is a most brilliant blue above and rich bay on the head and below, but the throat and breast are pure white, and there is a pure white patch on the pinion-quills. The bill and feet are scarlet, so that the whole effect is very brilliant indeed. The cock and hen are exactly alike, but young birds have the bill

PLATE VI.

One-half Natural Size.

1.—RED-CRESTED CARDINAL (Grey and white, scarlet head). 2.—BUDGERIGAR (Black and yellow above, green below). 3.—JAVA SPARROW (Blue-grey, black and white head, pink bill). 4.—GOLDFINCH (Brown, scarlet face, black and yellow wings).

and feet nearly black, and some dark fringes on the white breast.

This Kingfisher is found all over India, Burma, and Ceylon, but does not, as a rule, ascend the hills to any height. Outside India it extends from Cyprus to Cochin China, and in our limits it is a very common bird, found often in gardens and other places away from water, for it feeds on many other small creatures besides fish, including earthworms, insects, frogs, and even small birds. It has a slow undulating flight, and when it makes a swoop on a fish comes down in a very half-hearted way, unlike the determined plunge of the regular professional Kingfisher. When taking its tub, however, it will plunge with the best of them. I long knew a bird of this kind which haunted the tank in the Indian Museum grounds, and I regret to say I have known it guilty of piracy, as it took to robbing the dabchicks of the fish they caught.

This shows the bird objects chiefly to the trouble of catching fish, and he could probably be tamed by throwing out a few live ones for him on the grass. This would be a better way of establishing relations with such a bird than caging it, although, unlike most Kingfishers, it bears confinement very well. My friend Mr. E. W. Harper, had one for a long time in a cage, and it was in the most beautiful condition, but he is an exceptionally keen fancier, and spared no trouble.

This Kingfisher shows the manner of the origin of species very interestingly. In the Andamans, where it is very common, it is noticeably darker than in India, but similar specimens, chocolate instead of bay, now and then turn up on the mainland. Thus it would seem that the Andamans were originally stocked with a dark strain, or that the conditions of life there are easier for dark birds. It only needs the disappearance of the dark complexion among Indian specimens to establish the Andaman Kingfisher as a species, whereas now it has to rank as a variety only.

The White-breasted Kingfisher breeds from March to July and differs from other Kingfishers in occasionally making a rough nest of moss. But the birds that do this must be constructive geniuses of an uncommon kind for the ordinary squalid burrow is good enough for most of them. When courting they lift up their tails and droop their wings, showing off the white patch. At this time, too, they fly wildly about, uttering a peculiar wailing cry, whereas in the ordinary way their flight is direct, and announced in a most business-like way by an abominably harsh cackle; for this Kingfisher seems to think that his movements are of importance in local feathered society, and always gives due warning when he is making a change of quarters.

THE HOOPOES.

The Hoopoes are a small family of birds widely distributed over the Old World. They are all very much alike, having pale brown plumage with the wings and tail black-and-white, and their long thin bill and fan-like crest will always distinguish them from other birds, especially as the plumage does not differ with age and sex. The crest is ordinarily kept folded down and then looks merely pointed, but when the bird is angry or afraid or courting, or has just alighted, it is fully expanded and looks very pretty indeed. The wings are large and broad, and the flight is lazy and undulating, so that the bird looks like a big butterfly on the wing, but it is really a very strong and enduring flier. The legs are short, and the toes three before and one behind; the birds walk well and spend most of their time on the ground, pegging into it with their bills in search of the insects, etc., on which they feed.

They nest in holes, laying spotless eggs of a bluish or greenish-white and the hen sits very close, hardly ever coming off the nest. The said nest smells most vilely, the smell being either due to the extremely unsanitary state in which the interior is found, or to an exhalation from the birds themselves—"dirty as a Hoopoe" is a French proverb. With this exception, the Hoopoes are altogether charming birds; when not molested they are quite familiar, and come freely into gardens, where they are ornamental as well as useful. They are not sociable, going singly as a rule, but where they are found commonly they are quite a feature in the local bird-life, and are well-known to the natives under the name of *Hudhud.* They do not sing, but have a pretty double call like "hoop-hoop;" they also make a "swearing" noise when angry or frightened.

Hoopoes can be kept in confinement if reared from the nest, but are not very easy birds to keep. Hand-reared birds have been known to become so tame that they could be allowed full liberty, and in any case if confined it should be in an aviary, not in a cage. They do not care to bathe, but roll themselves in sand like Larks or Partridges, and they should always be given something, such as earth or turf, to dig their bills into. Two of the few species of Hoopoes known are found in India, and both are common birds, and probably not distinguished from each other by the casual observer.

THE EUROPEAN HOOPOE (*Upupa epops*). This bird is about a foot long, of which the bill measures more than two inches. The wings and back are banded broadly with black and white; the tail is black with a white crescent of which the convexity is towards the root; the belly is white with dark streaks and the rest of the plumage sandy buff, warming into cinnamon on the crest, which is tipped with black; but on the longest feathers there is a white space before the black tip.

This bird is found in summer all across the temperate parts of the Old World, migrating south in winter, at which time it is found in and about Calcutta. It only breeds with us in the Western Himalayas, in the months of April and May, laying from four to seven eggs. This is *the* Hoopoe *par excellence*, the subject of so many legends; for it has always attracted the attention of man from its curious appearance and gestures. The Romans knew it as *Upupa*, and the Greeks as *Epops*, so that its scientific name is most happily classical—a pleasing relief to the barbarisms of most scientific nomenclature. It visits England yearly, and has been known to breed there when allowed to live long enough, which is not often, as it is usually shot down on sight. It is a pity that some wealthy naturalist does not import a few dozen from the continent, and turn them loose, a proceeding which would have the effect of completely upsetting the value so absurdly placed on "genuine British-killed specimens," as then no one would know whether any Hoopoe appearing in England had got there naturally or not, and so the makers of the pettifogging "local records" would be quite at a loss.

THE INDIAN HOOPOE (*Upupa nigripennis*). This very closely resembles the European bird, but differs in being of a warm cinnamon where the other is buff; this colour also extends further, there being no white band before the black tip of the crest, and the reddish hue running further down the belly. Moreover, the wing is proportionately shorter in this species, and the bill often longer.

This Hoopoe is a resident bird, and is found nearly all over India, Burma, and Ceylon, except Sind and the Western Punjab; eastwards it extends to Hainan. It is not found in the vicinity of Calcutta, where Hoopoes are never common; but all those I have seen there, whether at large or brought into the New Market, have belonged to the last species. The habits of the Indian Hoopoe are the same as those of the Western bird; in India it may be found breeding from February to May, and in Ceylon from December to April. As some Indian specimens show a tinge of white on the crest, it is suspected that the two species interbreed, and this is extremely likely to be the case.

Before leaving the subject of Hoopoes, it may be as well to mention a legend about these birds which I found was known even to the natives in Calcutta; Charles Kingsley has familiarized English readers with it in "Westward Ho!" It seems that the Hoopoes had rendered a signal service to King Solomon, who thereupon offered them a reward. This they very foolishly chose to have in the form of golden crowns; but, on finding they were persecuted to the death for their unlucky jewelry, they came to the king to ask him to take back his gift. He saved his royal word by leaving them the crown, but changing it to one of feathers, which they have worn happily everywhere but in England, where the "enthusiastic local naturalist" cares not a jot for King Solomon! The Hoopoe was forbidden to the Jews as food, the word translated "Lapwing" in the Bible really meaning the Hoopoe; and when the ill-flavoured nest of the bird, and the dirty surroundings among which it often seeks its food are taken into consideration, the prohibition does not seem unreasonable.

THE SWIFTS.

These birds are usually confounded with Swallows both by Europeans and natives, and as they resemble them in form, and in their habits of seeking their insect food on the wing and resorting to buildings for nesting purposes, the error is natural. But examination of the anatomy of the birds has shown that while the Swallows are not to be separated from the ordinary Passerine birds, the Swifts present so many differences that they cannot be classed in that order at all.

Externally, Swifts may be distinguished from Swallows by the fact that they have only ten tail-feathers instead of the usual twelve, and in the case of the commonest species by the fact that the first toe is not directed backwards as in the Swallows; all the four toes spreading out like the fingers of the hand, or falling into right and left pairs.

As far as their habits are concerned, Swifts differ from Swallows, in most cases, by never settling on the ground or trees, etc. They do not perch or walk, but can cling or climb well enough, their claws being very strong and sharp. Their nests are built of various materials, stuck together by the abundant and viscid saliva of the birds, and the "edible bird's nests," so dear to the Chinese in more senses than one, are made by a small Swift (*Collocalia francica*) found in some localities on our coasts among other places, which uses nothing but the saliva in the construction, this drying into a substance like isinglass. The eggs of all Swifts are long and white.

Young Swifts are hatched naked, and fledge off into a plumage much like that of their parents. These seldom differ in plumage according to sex, nor has the male any song. They are not particularly interesting as birds go, but two are so common that they deserve notice here.

THE HOUSE-SWIFT (*Cypselus affinis*) is well over five inches long, and has a short square-ended tail; its plumage is sooty-black with a conspicuous white patch on the back, and the throat also white. Young birds are almost exactly like the old ones.

This bird is found almost all over Africa and India, but east of the latter country is replaced by a blacker species with the tail rather longer and slightly forked (*Cypselus subfurcatus*). It is sociable in habits, and builds in numbers in houses, making nests of any sort of light rubbish it can pick up on the wing, such as feathers, straw, etc. The materials are stuck together with saliva, and the nest varies in shape, and may be either in a hole or stuck to the roof.

Three eggs are usually laid, and two broods brought off in a year, the breeding-season lasting from February to August, and the birds resorting constantly to the same nest, which they also use for sleeping and resting, never perching outside. It has been said that these birds cannot rise from the ground, but this is a mistake; at least, in several experiments, I found only one uninjured bird that could not; birds that are obviously hurt are frequently found, for this Swift is constantly getting into difficulties by entering places whence it cannot readily escape; it seems to be a very stupid bird.

It has a clear shrill squeal, most frequently uttered before roosting time, when flocks of them career round and round before going to bed. It is not a migratory species, and in places where it is common, as at Calcutta, is one of the most conspicuous birds at all times. I doubt if it is advisable to encourage these birds where Swallows can be got to build, as they are not nearly so attractive as the latter, and are apt to drive them away in order to take their nests. But in default of the real Swallows, Swifts are better than nothing.

THE PALM-SWIFT (*Tachornis batassiensis*) is only a little less in length than the House-Swift, but is really a much smaller bird, being more slender, with a fairly long and well-forked tail; in colour it is drab, without any conspicuous markings.

It is found over a large part of India and in Ceylon, wherever the fan-or toddy-palm grows; it attaches its nest to the underside of the fronds of this tree, and does not stray far from it; for a Swift it is not at all a rapid flyer.

The nest is a small pocket, lodged in a furrow of the leaf, and made of vegetable fluff or small feathers stuck together with saliva. The bird occasionally makes use of the betel-nut palm, and is believed to breed twice in the year. In Northern India the times for breeding are March and July, but in Ceylon from October to April. Like the House-Swift, the Palm-Swift usually lays three eggs. East of India, throughout Burma to Java, is found another species of Palm-Swift (*Tachornis infumatus*) which is much darker, nearly black above, in fact. It has the same habits as the Indian bird, but in the Naga and Garo Hills frequents native huts, these being thatched with palm-leaves, to which the bird attaches its nest just as if they were on the tree.

THE NIGHTJARS.

These birds, often called Goatsuckers from an absurd superstition which was current even among the ancient Greeks and Romans, are easily distinguished from any others. They are birds of fair apparent size, but really very small and light in body, with large flat heads, long wings, and fairly long tails. Their beaks are very small indeed, and their mouths enormous, often with a row ot strong bristles along each side. Their feet are small, with three toes in front and a small hind-toe. The front toes are joined at the root by a small web, as in a fowl, the middle toe is furnished with a claw toothed like a comb on the inner side. The plumage is very soft, and beautifully stippled and mottled with various shades of brown and grey, so as to look like bark or earth; there is little or no difference between male and female; where there exists any, the young resemble the hen in their first plumage. They are covered with mottled down, and are soon able to run; but they do not feed themselves, being fed by the parents from the bill like the naked helpless young of many other birds. There is no nest at all, the eggs being simply laid on the bare ground; they are mottled so as to look like pebbles, and so escape observation.

The Nightjars feed entirely on insects, mostly caught on the wing, and are among the most useful of birds. Their flight is very light and graceful, and at night, the time of their activity, they are almost always on the wing.

By day they rest either on the ground or on a thick branch, on which they sit lengthways, not crosswise like other birds. Nightjars are found almost all over the world in warm and temperate regions, but are more often heard than seen, their notes being very peculiar and remarkable. They are commonly known in Hindi as *Chip-puk*, *Chappa*, *Dab-churi* or *Dabhak*.

THE COMMON INDIAN NIGHTJAR (*Caprimulgus asiaticus*). This bird is a little over nine inches long, and of a yellowish-grey colour above, splashed with black on the crown, and with fine black streaks on the back. There is a broken buff collar, and black and buff markings on the shoulders. Below the plumage is buff with indistinct brown bars, and a white spot on the throat. There are also white spots on the first four pinion-quills, and the outer two pairs of tail-feathers are tipped with white.

The shanks are completely bare to the hock, whereas in most of our Nightjars they are more or less feathered. The large eyes are dark, as is usually the case with these birds.

This Nightjar inhabits India, Ceylon, and Burma as far south as Moulmein, but it avoids high hills and large forests, keeping to the plains in cultivation and low jungle and even entering gardens. It is often known as the Ice-bird, from its note, which resembles the sound made by a stone flung upon ice and rebounding from it.

Its two eggs may be found, according to locality, at any time between April and September; they are about an inch long, faintly spotted with brown and purple on a pinkish-stone or salmon-coloured ground.

THE CUCKOOS.

Cuckoos are found all over the world, but are not numerous in species except in warm regions. They have slightly curved bills of moderate size, with conspicuous nostrils set low down and near the edge of the upper chap, and their toes are in two pairs, the outer front toe being turned backwards, as in Woodpeckers and Barbets. Tree-Cuckoos, which in the East at all events, lay their eggs in the nests of other birds, have long wings and short legs, while Bush-Cuckoos, which always bring up their own young, have short wings and long legs suited for running; the Tree-Cuckoos, on the rare occasions when they come to the ground, being only able to hop. Cuckoos usually have long rounded tails, and are very readily recognizable when a few have been seen.

The male and female are usually alike in plumage, but the young, which are hatched naked, are very different in first feather. Cuckoos have peculiar notes, and are generally more heard than seen. They generally feed on insects, and are exceedingly useful birds. Only in India are any Cuckoos commonly kept as cage-birds, the calls of our commonest species being much admired by the natives. They are not hard to rear, but require hand-feeding for a longer time than other birds.

THE KOEL (*Eudynamis honorata*). This species, called *Kokil* in Bengali, is the commonest and most familiar of Indian Cuckoos; it is found all over India, Ceylon and Burma, but does not ascend the hills above the warm zone. It is a familiar object wherever there are trees even in towns, and extends even to such outlying spots as the Laccadives; while its range to the Eastwards extends to Flores.

It is about as big as a large pigeon, with a long rounded tail; its whole length being nearly a foot and a half. It has a peculiar steady level flight, which makes it easily recognizable. The cock and hen differ absolutely in colour, the former being a glossy blue-black, while the latter is brown, spotted with white on the head and back, and barred with that colour on the wings, tail, and under-parts; altogether she rather reminds one of a hen pheasant in colour. Both male and female have pale green bills, bright red eyes, and lead-coloured feet.

Young birds have black bills and grey eyes; in plumage they resemble adults of the corresponding sex, but not completely, young cocks being usually slightly marked with buff, and young hens having the head and top of the neck black. But there appears to be some variation, so that young cocks may be found in female plumage, and *vice versâ*.

Unlike most Cuckoos, the Koel feeds on fruit entirely or almost so; and under the circumstances is probably rather an undesirable bird in a garden. It is, however, much beloved by natives, who admire its fine mellow call, and it is with them quite a bird of romance, the locks of beauty being compared to its glossy plumage. It deserves a certain amount of consideration from everyone, not only on account of its beauty and musical capacities, but for being one of the very few creatures which scores off the Crows, those birds being the foster-parents which it selects for its young. The House-Crow is the usual victim, and the egg of the Koel is a miniature of a Crow's egg, being about an inch long, and green with brown spots.

Sometimes two Koels' eggs may be found in one Crow's nest, and at times the big black Jungle-Crow has to do parental duty for the Koel. The most curious thing about the whole business is that the Crows, although they bring up the young Koel and feed it even after it has left the nest, yet evidently know there is something wrong, for they cherish a lively prejudice against the old Koels, and hunt any Koel they can to death if they get the chance.

The Koels breed from March to July, and at this time the call whence is derived its Hindustani name "ko-eel ko-eel," running up the scale, is one of the characteristic sounds of the country. Unfortunately the bird insists on calling at night as well as by day, and is rather apt at all times to be "instant out of season"; whence many Europeans call him the Brain-fever Bird, and detest him accordingly. The male, which has another call of his own, like "ho-e-o," is a favourite native pet, and seems to thrive well on satoo; like all Cuckoos, however, he is restless in a cage, and apt in this way to break and damage his plumage, though not so much as other species. In an aviary of the larger birds, a pair of Koels make a nice addition, but are hardly worth keeping in most places, as they are so common outside.

THE HAWK-CUCKOO OR "BRAIN-FEVER BIRD" (*Hierococcyx varius*), called *Popiya* by the natives, is a smaller bird, not much over a foot long, with much weaker bill and shorter legs than the Koel. The cock and hen are alike, blue-grey above, with tail barred with buff-edged dark bands, and below white on the throat and belly, and cinnamon on the breast, which is barred below. The eyes are bright yellow, the legs yellow, and the bill black above and greenish below.

The young bird is quite differently coloured, being brown above, barred with buff, and white with brown spots below; the eyes are grey at this stage.

In both stages the bird bears a most astounding resemblance in colour to the Shikra or common Sparrow-Hawk of India (*Astur badius*) in its corresponding plumages; and as the flight is also exactly like the Hawk's, it is difficult to tell the two birds apart unless one is near enough to see the difference in the beak. This, no doubt, is one reason why the Brain-fever Bird is so much better known by name than by sight.

It is really a very common bird, found over most of India and Ceylon, and ascending the hills up to seven thousand feet. But it is not found in Sind or the Punjab, and doubtfully in Assam and Burma. In Ceylon it is stated to be a migrant, arriving in November. Its note, so much disliked by Europeans, though natives like it, is variously rendered as "brain-fever, brain-fever, &c.,", running up the scale, or as "O lor', O lor', how very hot it's getting; I feel it, I feel it, &c." I prefer the last rendering, as it gives the preliminary notes by which the bird gets his pitch, as it were; moreover, the sentiment is appropriate, as the bird is specially noisy from April to June, its breeding season, when it calls even by night. Unfortunately, the bird's efforts at this season, when even the Nightingale would be a burden, are not appreciated, and would get a charge of shot as buckshot if the singer could be located—which he generally cannot. Those who are prejudiced against Brain-fever Birds should search the nests of the Satbhai or their relatives, for it is to these Babblers that the Hawk-Cuckoo entrusts her egg. As in the case of the Koel, the parasitic egg is like the legitimate one, being of course blue in this case.

The Hawk-Cuckoo feeds both on fruit and insects, and is frequently in Bengal, at any rate, reared as a cage-bird, but it always knocks itself about to the utter ruin of its plumage, and cannot be called a desirable pet. It should be fed on *satoo*, fruit and insects, and kept away from other birds, as these have the greatest dislike to it on account of its suspicious appearance.

THE COUCAL OR CROW-PHEASANT (*Centropus sinensis*). This is a very different bird from the parasitic Cuckoos above dealt with, and lives a most irreproachable life as far as attending to its parental duties is concerned. It is a big bird, over a foot and a half long, with a powerful bill and rather long legs, the inner hind toe being furnished with a long straight claw like a Lark's, whence the term "Lark-heeled" often applied to Cuckoos of this type. Its wings are short and round, and its tail very long ; the plumage is harsh and wiry, and the bird's general appearance quite justifies the name popularly given to it. It is known in Hindustani as *Mahoka.*

Cock and hen are alike in colour, being glossy blue-black with bright chestnut wings, black bills and feet, and bright red eyes. The young in first plumage have grey eyes, but vary a great deal in colour, some being dull editions of the parents, and others quite different. In these latter, the black parts of the plumage are closely barred with white and the wings barred with black. Such birds are always bigger than the others, and may be, as Jerdon says, the hens, since in this bird the hen is rather larger than the cock. But if this is so, it is curious that all the birds in a brood are either hens, or cocks—at any rate, I have never seen birds of the two types brought in together, which, one would think, they should be if the colour were merely a sign of sex.

The Crow-Pheasant is found all over India, Ceylon and Burma, but does not go any distance up the hills ; eastward it extends to the Malay Islands and China. It is a very common bird in India, and may often be seen by the railway, its red and black plumage conspicuous in its slow heavy flight; it is usually alone. It is active both on the ground and in trees, running well, and hopping actively amongst the boughs. It feeds on any small animals it can overpower, insects, small reptiles and so forth, and holds down its prey with one foot when tearing it. Among other things, it kills snakes, and should on this account be protected, although destructive to young game.

It usually breeds from June to August, but in South India earlier; the nest is a large round one of leaves, grass, &c., with a hole in the side, and placed in a thick bush or tree. There are usually three eggs, which are chalky white, and nearly an inch and-a-half long.

The young are easily reared on raw meat, cockroaches, &c. When fledged they will eat practically anything, and at any rate the barred ones make very nice pets. One I had used to go about the compound quite at liberty, and would always come to me to have its head scratched, although it violently resented being taken up. Mr. D. Ezra had one recently which he allowed at times to run about his room, when it was as friendly as a dog, and, like one, would sit contentedly at his side, even at night.

The quite young bird has a peculiar choking call when crying for food, like "guk-kop-kop." The note of the old ones is a kind of hoot "hoop, hoop," and, like the notes of Cuckoos generally, is heard more often than the bird is seen.

CHAPTER VII.

The Parrots and Pigeons.

The Parrots are so different from all other birds that all ornithologists are agreed in giving them an order to themselves. They vary a great deal in size and colour but are always easily recognized. Their beak is exceedingly short and thick, and very much hooked; the upper jaw being moveable as well as the lower, in order to give sufficient play under the circumstances. Their shanks are very short, and, like the toes, covered with many very small wart-like scales; the toes are in pairs, the outer front toe being turned backwards.

Most of them use the feet as hands, holding pieces of food in one while they eat it. Another very characteristic habit of Parrots, and one almost confined to them, is the use of the beak as a third leg in climbing; indeed, the way in which they clamber about the boughs is very characteristic. As a rule, they keep to the trees, and when on the ground move with an awkward waddle. They are good flyers, but the style of flight differs a good deal. Their nests are almost invariably in holes of trees, &c., without any lining; and the eggs are always pure white. The young are usually naked at first, and fledge off very like the parents. When small, they are fed by the old birds from the crop, and as they will gape for food, are easy to rear.

Parrots are found throughout the warm regions of the world, and a few even in temperate climates; but there are none wild in Europe, and only one in the United States. Only a few kinds are found in India, but many are imported from the Eastern Islands, Australia, and even South America, and are so well known as to have native names. Parrots, indeed, are the oldest and most universally popular of all pet birds, largely on account of their well-known power of imitating the human voice; and of late years it has been realized that the smaller species at all events are most admirably suited for aviaries.

As this work deals only with the birds of the garden and aviary, I shall not say anything about the large species of Parrots—Cockatoos, &c., commonly kept in cages; and in dealing with the aviary birds, I shall be compelled to limit myself to a few easily obtained and particularly desirable species, space not permitting to treat of all the many kinds imported. In keeping and handling Parrots, it must be remembered that they bite like rats, and they must by no means be associated with birds smaller than themselves; in fact, if their companions are bigger it will be just as well. With birds of their own order they get on fairly well, so that several kinds may be kept together; though not always if they are breeding.

For breeding accommodation, boxes with a small entrance hole or some other artificial cavity, should be provided. A section of an old log with a chamber hollowed out in it would be best of all, because most natural. Fortunately they seldom require animal food, so they are very easy to provide for; as most people must have observed, they crack all sorts of grain before eating it, and generally eat very slowly, like the Finches. No species of Parrot has as yet been thoroughly domesticated, though several are bred; but no one, however, he and she may object to keeping birds captive, need feel qualms of conscience about Parrots, for they are the most destructive of all birds to field and garden crops, and would have to be killed down if not caught for caging. The Parrots are divided into several families, examples of three of which are constantly to be had in India.

THE TYPICAL PARROTS.

The Typical Parrots form the largest family, such species as the well-known Grey Parrot of India, the Amazons and Macaws of America, and all our Indian Parrots, belonging to it. The small long-tailed kinds are called Parakeets or Parroquets. The Parrots of this family are hardly ever crested, nor do they have a brush tongue. They feed both on fruit and grain, and should only receive such food in captivity, sop or other soft food being avoided.

THE COMMON INDIAN OR ROSE-RINGED PARAKEET *Palæornis torquatus*). This well-known bird, called *Lybar Tota* in Hindustani, and *Tiya* in Bengali, hardly needs description, but it may be characterized briefly. It is about sixteen inches long, about ten of which belong to the tail; in colour it is green with a red bill and white eyes. The male has a black throat, the black running a little way on each side to join a rose-pink collar which extends round the back of the neck.

Young birds of both sexes are like the hen at first, having no collar, but their eyes are black, so that they can easily be distinguished from old ones.

Varieties of this Parakeet are not at all uncommon; many birds are found splashed with yellow, and now and then a pure yellow one turns up, which, if a male, retains the red collar. Both sexes of the yellow variety have a red bill, but their feet are flesh-coloured, instead of grey like those of the green birds. Their eyes are often pink; if this is not the case, they are liable to moult out into the ordinary green plumage. A pale yellow-green variety is also found, but seems to be very rare.

This species is found nearly all over India and Ceylon and extends east to Pegu; but it usually avoids the hills. It is much the commonest of Indian Parrots, and is far too familiar as a garden-bird, doing a great deal of damage to fruit. It even comes into towns, where its presence is unobjectionable, and gives an added touch of Orientalism to the scene, especially in Bombay where it is very numerous; in Calcutta it is not very common. It breeds from January to May, using holes in buildings as well as those in trees. Many birds are brought into the markets unfledged, and to secure and rear a few of these is the best way of getting a talker, as birds already instructed are naturally dear and hard to get. Young Parakeets are commonly fed in Calcutta on soaked lentils, and learn to feed remarkably early, especially when it is considered that they naturally do not leave their holes till quite fledged.

In an aviary these birds do well, and have bred in captivity in England; it would be worth trying the experiment in India in order to propagate the beautiful yellow variety. If specimens of this could not be got, careful breeding from heavily-splashed birds, such as can often be had in Calcutta cheaply, might very possibly produce it before long.

Some specimens of this Parakeet talk very well indeed; the only talking individual I have ever seen myself was a hen, so it would appear that sex does not matter much. It is almost the oldest foreign cage-bird known in Europe, as it was kept by the ancient Romans; the parrot whose funeral ode was written by Ovid was evidently a bird of this species, since the poet describes it as green with a red bill. A great many are sent to England yearly, and sold very cheaply.

A very similar species to the Ring-necked Parakeet is the bird commonly known to dealers as the Rock Parrot, and in books as the Alexandrine Parakeet (*Palæornis nepalensis*). This, however, is a much larger bird than the ordinary Ring-neck, and has, in both sexes and at all ages, a large dark red patch on the wing, which will distinguish it at once. It varies a good deal according to the district it inhabits, but the different varieties can hardly be ranked as species, though this is commonly done. Classing all these large Ring-necked Parakeets together, the Alexandrine may be said to be found almost all over India, Ceylon and Burma, and also extends to the Andamans, where it is very large and bright coloured. The only yellow specimen of this bird I have ever seen came from these islands, but it was not a very pure yellow. The Alexandrine Parakeet is known to the natives in Bengal as *Chandana.* and is very often kept by them.

There are several other Indian species of these green Parakeets, but the only one which we can notice here is THE BLOSSOM-HEADED PARRAKEET OR PLUM-HEADED (*Palæornis cyanocephalus*) called *Tuia* in Hindustani and *Faraida* in Bengali. This lovely little bird is not bigger than a Mynah in body, but its long tail makes it measure well over a foot. In colour the cock is mostly green, with a crimson head washed with blue, just like a ripe red plum; the long middle tail feathers are rich blue with white tips, and there is a small red patch on the wing. The bill is orange. The hen is very similar, but has a purple-blue head instead of a red one, and no red spot on the wing. Young birds are all green, but soon show colour on the cap; their small size and orange bills will easily distinguish them from young Ring-necks.

The Plum-head is found in Southern India and Ceylon, and right up to the lower slopes of the Himalayas. In the eastern part of this range it meets Rosa's Parakeet, or the Eastern Plum-head (*Palæornis rosa*) which is the common species in Burma. This differs from the Indian bird in having a much paler head, the male's being pink rather than crimson, more like a peach than a plum; the hen's head is paler and greyer than the Indian bird's and she has the red wing-spot like the cock. The most certain distinction (as some Indian males at all events have very pale heads) is that in the Indian Blossom-head the lining of the wing is a distinct blue-green, whereas the Burmese has the under side of the wing as pure a green as the upper.

The Burmese Plum-head seems to have much the same habits as the Indian, which is far more of a jungle-bird than the Ring-neck, though it sometimes comes into cultivated land and makes itself a nuisance.

It is even swifter on the wing than the Ring-neck, and has a much prettier note, which is too musical to be called a screech. It breeds from March to May; the Burmese bird's breeding-season is earlier in the year. Both species are fairly commonly sold in the Calcutta markets, but the Eastern or pale-headed birds are usually the commonest, though numbers of the true Indian Plum-head can be had at the beginning of the cold weather. It is, however, very scarce in the English market at the present time, though a good many of the Burmese species have been sent home, and this kind has been bred by Dr. A. G. Butler in an aviary.

As aviary birds these lovely Parakeets are particularly desirable, their beautiful colours, graceful form, and comparatively sweet notes being great recommendations. Yellow varieties are now and then to be seen, and those I have seen have generally had pink heads and red eyes; Mr. D. Ezra had a very beautiful specimen when I left India, but it was to my mind less handsome than a yellow Ring-neck which he also had.

THE ROSELLA (*Platycercus eximius*)* is a good example of the broad-tailed Australian Parakeets I mentioned in Chapter I. The figure (Fig. 3) on Plate VII will give some idea of its markings, but the actual bird is quite a revelation of vivid colour. The head, a patch under the tail, and the upper breast are scarlet, with the cheeks and throat pure white; the lower breast is yellow, and the back yellow and black; the wings and tail are rich purple-blue. The hen is nearly as bright as the cock, but has sometimes a green patch in the scarlet at the back of the head. The young show more of this, and are duller altogether, but still much resemble the parents, and cannot be mistaken for anything else.

This splendid native of Australia has long been exported from that country, and has been often bred in captivity in Europe. It may frequently be obtained in Calcutta, but is rather dear. It bears captivity very well, and will live for years even in a cage, though an aviary is far more suitable for such active birds as are these broad-tailed Parakeets. In such an abode the Rosella is seen to great advantage, as it constantly flies about, exhibiting its brilliant colours, and often uttering a pleasant note. Caged specimens occasionally talk, but this can hardly be recommended as one of the regular talking Parrots.

Occasionally one may obtain in Calcutta two other very lovely Parakeets allied to the Rosella, and much resembling it. These are the Mealy Rosella (*Platycercus pallidiceps*), which has a delicate pale yellow colour where the common bird is red, on the head and upper breast, and the lower breast a beautiful blue; and Pennant's Parakeet (*Platycercus elegans*) which is crimson and purple. The latter is a bigger bird than the other two, and almost entirely olive-green in its first plumage.

The Budgerigar or Undulated Grass-Parakeet (*Melopsittacus undulatus*)* is represented in Plate VI (Fig. 2). This and the brief description attached to the plate will give an idea of the colours and markings, and it may be added that the centre tail-feathers and some spots on the cheek are rich blue. Both sexes are alike in plumage, but in the male the cere, or naked skin surrounding the nostrils, is rich bright blue, and in the female pale blue or pale brown—in the latter case she is just ready to breed. Young birds are much like the old ones, but have dark eyes and the pencilling of the head continued all over the forehead.

This lovely little Parakeet, also known as Zebra Parakeet, Shell-Parrot, and Australian Love-bird, is, as the last name implies, a native of Australia. Indeed, the title Budgerigar, by which it is now generally known both in England and in India, is derived from the name "Betcherrygah" given to it by the Australian blacks.

It is sociable in habits, going in large flocks, and for about half a century vast numbers have been exported to Europe. Many also are sent to India, and they can generally be had in the Bird Bazaar at Calcutta at reasonable prices. Budgerigars are hardy and long-lived birds in captivity, and will sometimes breed even when a single pair are confined in a cage. The proper way to breed Budgerigars is, however, to turn about three pairs loose into a fair-sized aviary; as, unlike most birds, they breed better in company, being sociable even in the breeding season.

Cocoanut husks with an entrance-hole at one end should be fixed for them to breed in; for food they need merely canary-seed and millet, with a fresh sod of turf put in daily. So treated, they will multiply like the Sparrows, having up to five young at a brood; they are, in fact, the best and most certain breeders of all cage-birds, and will very much more than repay their original cost, keep, and housing, if any market at all exists for the young. They are much bred in Europe, and have been bred successfully in India, especially by Mr. F. Groser, who, starting with only one cock to three hens, bred a great number for years without any fresh blood. But this is the only case I know of where these birds have been allowed to revel in polygamy, and in-breeding is best avoided—though I am bound to admit that I only saw one unhealthy bird in all the numbers my friend had bred in this way.

In Europe a breed of yellow Budgerigars has been obtained, and specimens of this variety are now pretty generally for sale, though at three or four times the price of birds of the natural colour. One pair of these yellow birds I saw was absolutely pure yellow, with red eyes, but as a rule the eyes are of the natural colour —white with a black pupil—and the plumage, although yellow altogether at a little distance, shows on close inspection faint traces of the dark markings above, and a wash of green below. The blue cere and cheek-spots are as bright as in natural-coloured birds. Blue Budgerigars have even been obtained in two instances, the parents having been yellow ones.

It is evident that fanciers may yet do a good deal in the selective breeding of this charming little bird and this not only with regard to its colours, but its mental abilities also. Now and then a bird turns up which has an aptitude for imitating others ; I knew one which had learnt the song of an English Song-Thrush, and repeated it most accurately in a very pretty undertone. A few talking Budgerigars have even been recorded—hand-reared birds, of course ; and a more charming pet than a tame talking Budgerigar could hardly be imagined. Of course a talking or mocking specimen should always be bred from, if possible, as its offspring will probably show more than average ability in that line.

The Budgerigar is exceptional among Parrots in having a pretty little warbling chattering song of its own ; it is constantly exchanging remarks with its neighbours, but is never an unpleasantly noisy bird. As a companion to others, it is treacherous, and should never be associated, especially when breeding, with smaller and weaker birds. Birds bigger than itself, but harmless, such as doves, and the strong-billed Finches, such as Java Sparrows, are the best associates for it. The Javas and Budgerigars in particular look very well together, and, both being foot-biters, know what to expect from each other, and so remain fairly civil. A breeding Budgerigar, however, may be too much for the domestic happiness of even a Java Sparrow, and so plenty of extra nesting-places should be provided if the two species are kept in the same aviary.

Budgerigars are commonly trained by Italian women to " tell fortunes" ; that is to say, they are carried about the London streets in a cage, and for a penny fee will pull out a small sheet of prophecy concerning one's future. I argue from the "fortunes" told me by Budgerigars that I stand a good chance of living till 79, but as the bird once made a mistake, and gave me a lady's fortune, I am harassed by doubts as to their reliability as prophets. Our skilful native bird-trainers could probably do some remarkable things with these birds, since they show such docility.

THE LORIES.

These are a family of very pretty and active Parrots which live on fruit and the honey and pollen of flowers. To enable them to gather the last article of diet they have rather long tongues with a brush-like tip, with which they lick up their food. They are very swift on the wing, and much more nimble than ordinary Parrots among the boughs. On the ground they hop, instead of waddling like Parrots in general. Their bills are not quite so short and strong as Parrots' bills usually are, but they are nevertheless rather spiteful and mischievous with other birds, although naturally unable to bite so hard. They never have crests, and usually show a great deal of red in their plumage. A peculiar strong smell they have makes them unsuitable as indoor pets, and it is also a disadvantage that they must be fed on soft food, such as milk sop, soft fruit, &c., as like all such birds they are very dirty in a cage. This is a pity, as they are most tame and pettable birds, showing their affection more like a puppy than a bird, by tumbling and rolling about and playfully biting their owner's fingers.

If kept in a cage, therefore, this should be as large as possible; and the bird should be let out to have its bath, of which it is very fond. Fits are the chief cause of death among these birds, and plenty of exercise the best preventive. No sour food should be given under any circumstances. On the whole a big aviary where other strong soft food-eaters are kept is the best place for Lories. Many species are imported into India, but here we can only notice two, both of the green-backed sharp-tailed group known as Lorikeets or Loriquets.

The tiny short-tailed Bat-Parrots (*Loriculus*) are called Loriquets in the *Fauna of British India*; but this is not correct, as the birds, although feeding in the same way, have not brush-tongues, and do not belong to the Lory family. Moreover, since a Parrot with a sharp tail is called a Parakeet, the corresponding term Lorikeet ought surely to be restricted to the sharp-tailed Lories. The term Bat-Parrot is also an excellent name for the *Loriculi*, as these birds are unique in sleeping hung up by one foot, like the Bats among beasts.

FORSTEN'S LORIKEET (*Trichoglossus forsteni*).* This species, a native of the island of Sumbawa, was, in my time, about the most numerously imported Lory in Calcutta. The figure (Fig. 1) and brief description on Plate VII will give a sufficient idea of it; a band across the belly is purple as well as the head, and the pale collar is of a light shade of green. Cock and hen are alike, and the young are, I believe, similar. This handsome and lively bird does well in captivity, and has even been bred in the Calcutta Zoological Garden, the eggs being laid in an ordinary pigeon-box.

A still better Lorikeet, the Blue Mountain Lory of Australia (*Trichoglossus swainsoni*) is occasionally imported, and much resembles Forsten's. It has, however, the head and belly intense violet instead of purple, the red breast shading into yellow at the sides, and the tail much longer. This bird will eat seed as well as soft food, and is the easiest to keep of all Lories.

THE HARLEQUIN LORIKEET (*Trichoglossus ornatus*)* from Celebes, Buton and Togian Islands, is the liveliest and gayest of all the Lories imported. The arrangement of his colours may be gathered from the figure on Plate VII (Fig. 4); the red breast is barred with purple, and the collar is bright yellow. There are also some yellow markings on the green of the upper back and of the belly. The sexes are alike, as is always the case with Lories.

The great activity and brilliant colours of this bird make it a very striking ornament for an aviary and an interesting cage-bird. As the male, at any rate, is of a very amorous description, it would probably not be difficult to breed the species in captivity in so favourable a climate for these tropical birds as India presents.

THE COCKATOOS.

These are large short-tailed Parrots as a rule, always with some sort of a crest and with the plumage chiefly white, black, or grey, varied with red and yellow. They

PLATE VII.

One-quarter Natural Size.

1.—FORSTEN'S LORIKEET (Green; scarlet breast, purple head). 2.—COCKATIEL (Grey and white, yellow head). 3.—ROSELLA (Scarlet head, yellow breast, blue wings and tail). 4.—HARLEQUIN LORIKEET (Green; purple cap, red face and breast).

are grain-eaters, very easy to keep, and many are imported into Calcutta, where they are usually chained or caged. An aviary would have to be very strong to hold them, as they have most powerful beaks, which they are always burning to use. As, therefore, they are rather out of the scope of the present work, I shall confine my remarks to the only small and long-tailed member of the family which bears much the same relation to the big Cockatoos as the Parakeets do to the big short-tailed Parrots.

THE COCKATIEL (*Nymphicus novæ-hollandiæ*).* The general shape, size and colours of this bird may be gathered from the figure (Fig. 2) on Plate VII. The spot on the cheek is bright orange-red, and is present in both sexes. But the female differs from the male, which is the sex figured, in having the rest of the head olive instead of yellow, and in having the side feathers of the tail barred with black and yellow, instead of plain black as in the cock. She is thus very easily distinguishable, and the young of both sexes resemble her at first.

The form of the Cockatiel is particularly slender and graceful, and this is well shown by its very close and neat-looking plumage. It is, as might be expected from its long wings, a strong and graceful flier, and more active on the ground than most Parrots, being a ground-feeder in its native country, Australia. There it is often called the "Joey" on account of the red patch on the cheeks, like a clown's decorations. The name "Joey" is also applied to the Rosella, presumably because, like the Biblical Joseph, it has a coat of many colours.

The Cockatiel has been for many years much exported from Australia, and is a great favourite in Europe, as it breeds more freely than any other Parrot except the Budgerigar. It can generally be had also in Calcutta at a reasonable price, and is equally ready to breed in captivity there; a solitary hen will even lay in a cage.

In the Calcutta Zoological Garden a pair bred in a small aviary where they had for companions a pair of African Spotted Pigeons (*Columba guinea*) and an English Song-Thrush. Of the latter they took no notice, but the male was constantly attacking the Pigeons, although they were twice his size, and easily beat him off with their wings. This was while the sitting and rearing was going on; when the young Cockatiels came out fledged the Pigeons had their revenge, and pecked one nearly to death. Another pair of Cockatiels in another compartment showed themselves very unfriendly to a pair of Red-crested Cardinals confined with them; so that the temper of these birds is evidently not trustworthy in Bengal, where tempers generally are apt to give way on a slight strain. In England the Cockatiel has the reputation of being the gentlest of all Parrots, so that it can safely be kept with the smallest Finches.

A young male Cockatiel taken from the nest and reared by hand makes a delightful pet; it will learn to talk, and become so tame that it can be let out to fly about in the open. Altogether, next to the Budgerigar, the Cockatiel is the most desirable of all aviary birds, and is one of those which are practically certain to give satisfaction, and so eminently suited for the beginner in aviculture.

THE PIGEONS.

Pigeons form a family of birds which are found all over the world, and, like Parrots, are very distinct from all others, so that they are given an order to themselves. Their characteristics are easily seen in the common tame Pigeon—the weak bill, soft and swollen over the nostrils, the small head, powerful wings, and heavy body clothed in close powdery plumage. The feet are also very noticeable, with three toes before and one smaller one behind, a single row of scales down the front of the shank, and none at all at the back, which is covered with soft skin. Most Pigeons have red or purple feet, a few yellow ones.

Pigeons build very slovenly nests of twigs or dry grass, generally on the bough of a tree, but sometimes, like the tame Pigeon, in holes. They never lay more than two eggs, and the young from these are usually cock and hen. The eggs are always white or—very rarely—faintly tinted, and never show any spots.

The young are hatched blind and nearly naked, and are very ugly helpless little things, with swollen soft beaks. They do not gape for food like most young birds, but put their bills into that of the old one, which thereupon throws up the food from its crop, and lets them suck it in. The proverbial "Pigeons' milk" really does exist as a matter of fact, for during the first few days of their lives the young Pigeons are fed on a secretion from the crop of the old birds, which much resembles milk in appearance and chemical composition. Later this is mixed with softened grain, until at length the old birds give the young the grain almost at once, merely keeping it in their crops till they have got enough of it.

Grain of various kinds is, as everyone knows, the favourite food of most Pigeons, but as they cannot always get it, they eat a good deal of green food and a few small snails as well. A good many species, however, are fruit-eaters, and never touch grain. These have stouter beaks and shorter shanks than the grain-eating Pigeons.

Pigeons are strong fliers, and use their powerful wings in fighting, their beaks being so weak, although they can do each other a good deal of harm with them if too closely confined. For, in spite of their reputation for gentleness, they are inveterate fighters in a petty nagging way. To birds other than their own family, however, they are usually quite harmless. This makes them very desirable as aviary birds, for they can be kept with birds of other families smaller than themselves. They breed very readily in confinement, and are easier to manage than any other birds; both parents sit and feed the young, and need no special food when breeding.

It is, however, in most cases almost impossible to tell the cock from the hen, as their plumage is exactly similar; the young are rather different in many cases. The actions of the cock when courting are very interesting and differ much in the different groups.

Pigeons are not usually migratory, and are most numerous in a hot climate; there are many wild species in India, of which only a few can be noticed here. In addition to the common domestic Pigeon, which is descended from the wild Blue Rock Pigeons of Europe and

India (*Columba livia and intermedia*), the only other domesticated Pigeon is kept in India. Doves are known as *Fakhta* in Hindustani and *Ghughu* in Bengali.

THE COLLARED TURTLE-DOVE OR TAME RING-DOVE (*Turtur risorius*).* The wild stock of this very well-known pet bird appear to be the *Turtur roseogriseus* of North-East Africa. It is a graceful, rather long-tailed, bird, about a foot in length, of a pale delicate fawn colour, with a black crescent on the back of the neck, and the root half of the tail-feathers black underneath; the tips of all but the centre tail-feathers are white, and the pinion-quills drab. The eye is deep red with white eyelids, and the legs crimson in old birds and light pink in young ones, which have hardly any collar, and noticeably dull and cloudy-looking plumage. There is a pure white variety, in which the eye is yellow with a red pupil, and the beak flesh-coloured instead of black. Now and then also, birds may be seen of a paler fawn than usual, with drab instead of black on the neck and under the tail, and white pinion-quills and side tail-feathers. These would appear to be a cross between the white and coloured varieties, and Mr. Ezra tells me he has bred similar birds in this way. But in a case where Mr. J. Bathgate crossed a young fawn male with an older white hen, the young were ordinary fawn-coloured birds. This dove does well either in a cage or in an aviary, but, like all Doves, can only take proper exercise and show itself off in a large space. In either case, it breeds more freely than any other cage-bird, keeping on laying and rearing young continually.

Overcrowding, however, must be guarded against, or the birds will spoil each other's appearance by continual fighting.

The male when courting, inflates his neck and bows to the female, dragging his closed tail on the ground, and uttering a note like "coo-kur-roo," which to me is very pleasing, though some people find it painfully monotonous, as the bird coos a great deal even when not "playing up" to the female. She also coos, at any rate when alone. This Dove also has a nasal laughing note, uttered whenever it settles on a perch, and also by the male when pursuing the female before he settles down to coo to her. At such times he hops instead of walking in the usual way, and runs the last laugh into the first coo in the most ridiculous way, trying to say two things at once!

The general shape and courting positions of the wild Turtle-doves are very similar; they may also often be seen to fly up straight into the air for a few yards and come sailing down again with wings and tail outspread, a very pretty feat which the domestic bird practically never has a chance of performing, although I have seen a very tame old cock I had in England do it when I let him out in the open. But letting out birds like these would be too risky an experiment in India.

THE WILD RING-DOVE (*Turtur risorius*) bears a very great resemblance to the tame bird, but is considerably darker in colour, being drab instead of pale fawn, running into pinkish grey on the head and neck. It is about the same size, but slightly more delicate in form, and altogether certainly looks as if it might well be the ancestor of the domestic kind. But it has a distinctly different coo, and does not, so far as I know, ever utter the characteristic laughing note of the other.

This is one of the commonest birds over most of India and Ceylon, but is rare in Burma; it has a very wide range outside our limits, to Central Asia, Turkey, and China. In Yarkand it is a regular town bird, and in India is a common garden-bird in most places. About Calcutta, however, this is not the case, the species being rare, if found at all.

THE RED DOVE (*Œnopopelia tranquebarica*) is a small species, with the tail shorter in proportion, even to its size, than most Turtle-doves; its length is thus only about nine inches. The hen is drab with a black crescent on the back of the neck and white tips to the side tail-feathers. She thus looks very like a miniature wild Ring-dove, but the difference of size is too great for any real confusion to arise.

The cock Red Dove is very different from any other species, and even from his own hen, a remarkable case in this family. He is of course of the same size and shape as she is, and he also has the same black collar and white tips to the side tail-feathers, but his body colour is altogether different, being of a pinkish brick-red—about the shade that ladies used to call "crushed strawberry" a few years ago. His head and centre tail-feathers are of a delicate ash grey, well setting off the red.

Young cocks are drab, like the hens, at first. This beautiful Dove has a very gentle innocent appearance, its eyes being large and intensely dark, set off in many cases by dark grey eyelids. In some specimens, however, the eyelids are pink. The feet are deep purple, not red or crimson as doves' feet usually are.

This Dove cannot be called very common in India, though it is widely spread over that country, and extends to Burma, China and the Philippines. It is also found in the Andamans, but is very rare in Ceylon. I have only seen it wild myself in Dehra Dun—a remarkably good place for Doves; and I introduce it here as a particularly desirable aviary bird. The unique colouring of the cock makes him most ornamental, and the difference between the sexes makes it easy to select a true pair, thus doing away with the leading difficulty in breeding Doves. The Red species is a particularly free breeder; we had a pair in the Calcutta Zoological Garden which bred successfully in a large cage much less than six feet square, which they shared with other Doves of the same and other species, and a lot of other birds! It has also bred in the London Zoological Garden, and would be much appreciated by amateurs in England, where it is very rare as yet.

To people who dislike the monotonous and penetrating coo of most Doves, but admire the family nevertheless, this bird may be confidently recommended. It can only express its amorous feelings by muttering, which may not be romantic, but is not annoying to a third party! I once had a cream-coloured male of this species, which Mr. Rutledge gave me; except for its pale grey head, it was almost an exact miniature of the domestic bird. Like most Turtle-doves, the Red Dove seems to breed at almost any period of the year, but its eggs are not perfectly pure white, but tinted with cream-colour.

THE SPOTTED DOVE (*Turtur suratensis*) is the opposite of the Red Dove as regards proportions, having a decidedly long tail and short wings. It is a little smaller than the Ring-dove. Its colouring is not very easy to describe, but quite unmistakable; the general hue is pinkish, running into grey on the head; there is a large black patch dotted with white on the back of the neck, and the wings and back are drab, spotted with pinkish fawn-colour; the four centre tail-feathers are brown, the rest mostly black with white tips. Cock and hen are exactly alike, but the young are very dull and brown, without any black and white tippet and showing merely traces of the pretty mottling on the wings. The eyelids in old birds are pink-red.

This Dove is found all over India and Ceylon, and as far east as Manipur; in Burma it is replaced by the Malay Spotted Dove (*Turtur tigrinus*), which ranges east to Celebes. This species is less fully and distinctly spotted, and has dark grey eyelids, but otherwise is very similar.

The Indian Spotted Dove is the common Dove about Calcutta; it is a familiar garden-bird, quite common even in the town, and very tame, even coming on to verandahs. On my own, I saw one of these Doves attack and buffet a Crow, which fled ignominiously before it.

Like other Doves of this type, it breeds at all times of the year. It seems to be a very quarrelsome bird, and two may often be seen having a vigorous set-to, springing up and buffeting each other in the air. Its note is in three syllables, but rather hard to describe. Like other Doves, this species revels in heat; I have seen them at mid-day in May sunning themselves on the grass!

THE LITTLE BROWN DOVE (*Turtur cambayensis*). This pretty little Dove resembles the Ring-dove in form, but is only about ten inches long, and very dainty and graceful in appearance. Its general colour is brown, tinged with pink on the head, neck, and breast; the belly is white, and there are the usual white tips to the side tail-feathers. The neck is mottled with black in a very characteristic manner.

This Dove is common throughout the Indian Peninsula from the base of the Himalayas, and extends west to Arabia. But it is not found in Lower Bengal or in Ceylon, and is rare on the Malabar Coast. It is a very tame bird, coming freely into gardens, and has a particularly pretty soft laughing coo.

THE BRONZE-WING DOVE (*Chalcophaps indica*), called *Ram ghughu* or *Raj ghughu* in Bengali, is a bird of somewhat different type from the Turtle-doves, with a quite short tail, and standing higher on its legs than Pigeons generally—somewhat like a Partridge, in fact.

In colour the male is pinkish-chocolate with metallic bronze-green wings, a grey cap, and white forehead and eyebrows; the eyes are large and dark; the bill bright coral-red, and the feet dark crimson.

The hen is very similar, but can easily be distinguished, having the brown parts of the plumage less rich in colour, no grey cap, and the forehead and eyebrows grey instead of white.

The young are very different from either, being mostly dull brown above, barred with cinnamon, and with dusky below; but their characteristic shape, with this marking, will distinguish them. In length the bird measures only a little over ten inches, but is stout for its size, and about as big in body as the Spotted Dove.

It has a very wide range, from Mussoorie east through Burma and the Malay Islands to New Guinea, but is decidedly local in India itself, being found only in the lower Himalayas, Bengal, the forests near the Malabar Coast, and those between the Ganges and the Mahanuddy. It likewise inhabits the Andamans and Nicobars, and Ceylon, where it is called *Nila Kobeya.* It is a jungle bird, but sometimes comes into gardens.

I have only seen it wild in Dehra Dun, and have noticed there what authors have recorded of it—its solitary habits and low swift flight. It has a soft, long, plaintive note, said to be very soothing to one ruffled in his temper. Unfortunately the bird's own temper, as might be inferred from its unsociable ways, is anything but good, and in captivity it is given to bullying other Doves. For a good-sized aviary, however, it is a very nice bird. As it is a ground-dweller and active on its feet, its beautiful colours are well displayed, and the difference of the sexes is another recommendation. In the wild state it breeds during the first half of the year, and is thought to have two broods in this time; it builds a neater nest than most Doves, and lays cream-coloured instead of white eggs, thus keeping up its distinctness *ab ovo*. Specimens can often be bought of the Calcutta dealers.

THE CRESTED DOVE (*Ocyphaps lophotes*)* is a native of Australia, and frequently exported both to Europe and India. In size and general form it resembles the tame Ring-dove, but has a longer tail and legs, and a long pointed crest. Its general plumage is grey, running into dull pink down the sides of the neck; the back and wings are brown barred with black, and with broad white-tipped purple-bronze bands on the latter, much like the wing-bar of a duck. The long crest-feathers are black, and the tail black, glossed with purple and tipped with white. The eyes are orange with pink eyelids, and the feet coral-red. The cock and hen are exactly alike, but the young are much duller and have no gloss on the wings. They are fledged and leave the nest and fly about when quite small, only about half the size of the parents.

This, to my mind the most beautiful and interesting of all Doves, is a most excellent aviary bird; but, though it will live and breed well even in a small aviary, needs a large space to show itself properly. If this be given, it will be found far more lively and active than Doves generally, running almost as quickly as a Partridge, and flying rapidly, though with a whirring noise. When settling, it jerks up its tail perpendicularly. When courting the hen also, it erects and spreads its tail, and, slightly expanding its beautiful wings, pursues her with the most absurd courtesies and a not very musical coo. So strong and rapid on the wing is it, that if turned out in the open, I feel sure it would be esteemed by sportsmen as a useful minor game-bird.

The last Pigeon I shall deal with is a representative of the beautiful group of green Fruit-Pigeons, so characteristic of the warm regions of the old world.

THE HURRIAL (*Crocopus phœnicopterus*) is about as big as a common domestic Pigeon, but stouter in make, with the wings, tail, and legs shorter. Its bill is stout and strong for a Pigeon's. Its plumage is soft and extremely beautiful; the general colour being a yellowish-green, becoming almost yellow on the neck and breast; the underparts below this, the back of the head, a collar round the neck, and the end of the tail, are French grey. There is a narrow yellow stripe across the wings, and the thighs are yellow; at the bend of the wing is a lilac patch, and a buff-and-chestnut one under the tail. The bill is bluish-white, greenish at the root; the feet are orange yellow, and the eyes blue with an outer ring of red. The hen is very like the cock, but slightly smaller and usually with less of the pale purple on the wing; but the sexes are not easy to distinguish in this species.

This, the common Green Pigeon of Bengal and Burma, is found eastwards as far as Siam; to the west it extends along the base of the Himalayas to the Jumna, but in Northern India it meets the Southern Hurrial (*Crocopus chlorogaster*) of the Indian Peninsula and Ceylon. This bird, in its typical form, is all greenish-yellow beneath, showing no grey on the belly;

on the other hand there is no green on the forehead and root of the tail, the head and tail being all grey. Where the two kinds meet they appear to interbreed freely, as any number of intermediate specimens occur; and as the extreme forms only differ in the points of colour I have mentioned, they can perhaps better be called local varieties than really distinct species.

These Green Pigeons are sociable birds, being generally seen in flocks; they feed only on fruit which is small enough to swallow whole, such as banyan figs, and so are not destructive in gardens like most fruit-eating birds. Although not rare, they easily escape notice, as their plumage matches the foliage of trees so beautifully that they are almost impossible to see. They very seldom come to the ground; indeed, there is a native story that the Hurrial is so proud of never treading the vulgar earth that it carries a twig in its feet when it comes down to drink! If it is really proud, it certainly must be ashamed of its appearance on the ground, where it walks awkwardly like a Parrot, not with the dainty tripping gait of ordinary Pigeons. Among the branches, however, it moves gracefully and easily, and is so strong in the feet that it can reach over till its head is pointed perpendicularly downwards when it desires to pick a fruit below its perch. Hurrials build scanty open nests like ordinary Pigeons, and lay the two usual white eggs. In courting, they do not make so much fuss as Pigeons in general, merely stooping, expanding their tail and moving it up and down. Their note is not in the least like a coo, being a modulated whistle, and they are said sometimes to be kept for their song. They will live well in confinement, but of course need soft food. Boiled rice or other grain, or boiled vegetables cut up, will suit them very well, with any small fruits that can be got; with an occasional feed of plantain worked up with *satoo* into a crumbly paste. Fresh-caught birds should have plantains cut up into bits; but as soon as possible the plantain should be mixed with rice or *satoo*, since it is too messy and sticky if given alone. Fed in this way all these green Fruit-Pigeons are easy to keep; and as they are very rare in Europe, are always worth taking home.

Hurrials are themselves very good to eat; but when one comes to the table qualities of birds, we approach the domain of the sportsman; and as game-birds are barred in this little work, the Hurrial, which appeals both to the shikari and the aviarist, is a fit bird with which to close the series.

CHAPTER VIII.

Management of Captive Birds.

Aviaries.

The best place in which to keep and study birds is undoubtedly a garden aviary. In such a building they seem very contented and happy, live long and frequently breed, and give very little trouble; daily attention to the feeding and a weekly cleaning being all that is absolutely required.

Such an aviary should consist of two portions—a perfectly sheltered house, where the birds can be secure from hot sun, rain, and driving wind; and an outdoor enclosure of wire-netting, in which they can bask and exercise at pleasure.

The best way of making such an aviary, where facilities exist, is to partition off with wire-netting one end of a north verandah on the ground floor, and outside to erect a masonry platform as high as the verandah floor, on which should be placed one of those iron structures sold as plant-houses. When this has been netted over the birds can go in and out as they please, and they and their owner can enjoy the shelter of the verandah together when the weather is objectionable out-of-doors.

Of course such an ideal arrangement is often impossible. When there is no room in the compound for an outdoor "flight," a wire-netting bow-window should be made to project from the birds' end of the verandah, if possible, as complete exposure to the elements, when they wish it, is most beneficial for birds. Some Parrots, for instance, will only bathe in the rain. If there is no suitable place in the verandah, but plenty of room in the compound, a small octagonal house should be built outside, and the wire flight arranged round it; the house should be open on the north side, and its roof well thatched to secure coolness. Or the house may be built against a north wall, and a long wire plant-house put in front of it. But house and flight should always be on a masonry platform three feet high, to exclude damp and vermin.

The wire-netting also should never be more than an inch in mesh, and for birds smaller than a Pigeon half-inch mesh is necessary.

The flight should be turfed and planted with shrubs, which are best in pots.

Moveable Verandah Cages.

These are often called aviaries, but this term is best restricted to the fixed structures described above. Cages like these are very convenient, and birds of a Sparrow's size or less live very well in them. They are generally, however, made far too small. They should never be less than three feet every way, and should always be supported on legs three feet high. The roof should be gabled or pyramidal, and always of wood, not of netting, so that the birds may not be terrified by enemies above them. If vermin are very troublesome, the wire-netting should be double, the two layers being kept an inch apart by corks fixed between at intervals. Upright wires should never be employed, as birds are never really safe behind these, but may be torn through.

Cages for single birds.

These should always be oblong, so as to allow of two perches being put in a good distance apart and on the same level; in this way the bird can get good exercise by hopping to and fro. Bird-cages are usually cruelly small; a bird the size of a Canary requires a square foot of space, and others in proportion. The floor of all cages should have a moveable tray to facilitate cleaning, and the perches should be removeable for the same reason.

Perches.

These are often put in in a very haphazard way, but care in their selection is well repaid. For large aviaries natural branches of trees or bamboos, with plenty of twigs, are the best. For moveable aviary-cages branches also do well, if the door of the cage be large enough to put them in; the door of any cage should always be big, and closed by sliding, not with hinges.

A row of wooden hat-pegs fixed up against the side makes an excellent set of perches for an aviary or large cage. In either of these some perches should always be near the roof, so that the birds may roost well out of sight of anything which might disturb them.

Long straight perches should be avoided, as these offer a temptation to selfish birds, which can easily run along such and keep others off them.

The two perches in a small cage should always be round, and of different thicknesses, so as to ease the bird's feet by a change of grip.

NESTING PLACES.

In large aviaries and even in big cages many birds breed, and accommodation for nesting will be necessary. This must of course depend on the habits of the birds. Those that nest in holes, like Parrots or Mynahs, need small boxes, kegs, gourds, or in the case of small species, cocoanut husks, with a hole at one end for entrance, and a short perch projecting below it.

Those which nest in bushes, such as Finches, will be well pleased with small wicker cages, of which the door has been removed; or a natural bush with plenty of twigs will tempt them.

Doves, which build an open platform of twigs, are glad to have trouble saved them by being given a shallow open basket.

Nesting materials—twigs, short lengths of straw and hay, fine shavings, dry moss, feathers, and short hair—should be supplied according to the species of birds kept. The lighter and looser materials should be tied up in a little net, to keep them from being blown away and thrown recklessly about.

Many birds like to sleep in holes; miniature pigeon-boxes and even cocoanut shells—as opposed to husks—will suit these.

CLEANING.

Cages, whether large or small, should be cleaned daily and have the floor-tray covered with dry sand or earth; the very fine gravel which can be collected from roads after a shower is very good.

Aviaries need not be cleaned out so often, though if the indoor end be in a verandah, a daily cleaning is best. The bedding in an aviary should be thick if not renewed daily, and may be of sand, mould, dead leaves, or saw-dust. Dead leaves will amuse the birds and come in handy for the garden after. No aviary should be kept longer than a week uncleaned, unless shy birds are breeding in it.

The flight will of course not need cleaning, but may be turfed when the grass is getting thin.

Once a year all aviaries and large cages should be white-washed inside. All perches and nesting-boxes should be removeable, though securely fixed, so as to be cleaned at this time or oftener.

FEEDING AND DRINKING-VESSELS.

For aviaries and large cages shallow open pans are best, proportioned to the size of the inmates. The water-pan should be large as the birds will bathe in it; it should be unglazed, so that they can find good footing on the floor of it. In the outdoor aviary it should be placed on the turf in the flight; in a verandah cage on a sod of turf put in purposely; the splashing of the birds will keep the grass fresh for some time.

Food-pans should have the edges flanged over to keep the birds from throwing the food about; an enamelled iron spittoon, with the centre moveable piece removed, makes an excellent feeding-dish. If mice are troublesome in an outdoor aviary, and no ground-birds are kept, the food-dishes should be put on little tables, or hung up in wire flower-baskets. Food-vessels should be put indoors. Food or water-vessels should never be stood directly under a perch, to avoid fouling.

In small cages for single birds, the food- and water-vessels should always be placed inside, not outside, as is sometimes done with Europe-made cages. The receptacles should be little cups, held in place by a peg passed through the handles, which are put between the wires of the cage. The Chinese-made cups with curved sides and a narrow mouth are best, as preventing waste. A cage-bird's bath should be given to it in a separate larger vessel every morning before the cage is cleaned out, to avoid mess.

Food and Water.

These should always be looked to *daily* without fail. The water is best renewed in the afternoon as well as the morning, as birds often like to bathe twice a day, and much enjoy clean water.

Seed-eating birds are of course fed on various kinds of grain; if larger than a Mynah, paddy and corn of similar size may be given, as well as millet and canary seed as a treat. For birds smaller than a Mynah the small seeds will form the staple food, but such larger grains as they are found able to eat may also be given as a change. Thus, even the little Munias can husk paddy, and Canaries will appreciate a few oats.

Fruit-eating birds can be fed on plantain and other fruits, varied with bread-and-milk sop, boiled rice and vegetables, and *satoo* (gram-flour) made up into a crumbly paste with water As they are gross feeders and apt to get too fat, the more of their natural fruit diet they get the better they will live. Insect-eating birds, if smaller than a Mynah, should be fed on *satoo* worked up into a crumbly paste with ghee and hard-boiled eggs. These small species require live insects constantly, and there is a class of professional maggot-breeders and grasshopper-catchers in Calcutta who live by feeding Shamas for their owners.

Insect-eating birds of a Mynah's size or larger can be fed on scraps from the table cut up, much as one would feed a dog; or they may be given a standing dish of boiled rice mixed with chopped raw meat, or *satoo* worked into a crumbly paste with this. Cockroaches and crickets will be suitable insects to give these; and Jays, Magpies, &c., need dead mice and young Sparrows as often as these can be procured. Shrimps are very good for all insectivorous birds large enough to eat them.

As a matter of fact, many insectivorous birds also eat and need fruit, Starlings and Thrushes for instance; and these are naturally by far the easiest to keep. The purely insectivorous kinds should not be kept by anyone who cannot command a *constant* supply of live insects.

Green food, such as the various salad vegetables, is needed by seed-eating birds, and may be sometimes eaten by insect-eaters. If these do not naturally eat any salad or fruit when offered, it is well to mix a little finely-mixed lettuce in their paste, to make up for the green stuff which they swallow inside caterpillars. Green food for seed-eaters should be securely tied up, not thrown in. A few birds commonly kept are Honey-suckers to some extent. They should have sweetened sop or *satoo*-pap allowed them, but nothing sticky. Extreme care should also be taken not to give sour food to any bird. In reason. the more varied sorts of food a bird can be got to eat the better; but it should never be kept long on any artificial food exclusively, and its diet should never be suddenly changed altogether.

The idea that birds always know what is good for them is a mistake; they will over-eat themselves disgracefully. A bird which has not had fruit, green food or insects for some time should only receive such food sparingly at first, or it will make itself very ill, or even die outright.

Grit. Lime and Salt.

All seed-eating birds, and a good many others, need grit, such as coarse sand or fine gravel stones, to help in the digestion of their food. This should be given separately in a box if the aviary is not bedded with sand or earth. Only a very sparing allowance of grit should be given to birds which have not had it of late, or they will take too much, which often causes their death.

Lime is needed by hen-birds when laying, in order to form the egg-shell, and is beneficial to birds at all times. The best form in which it can be supplied to small birds is cuttle-fish bone, which can be obtained from a chemist, or picked up on the beach if one happens to live near the sea. The "bone" which is brittle and spongy, should be securely fastened up by a wire in reach of the birds, which gnaw it with great pleasure. Plaster rubbish from old houses is also useful.

Rock-salt is relished by Doves and Parrots, and a lump may be kept constantly in their reach.

Rearing young Birds.

This is very troublesome, as the little things require such frequent feeding; "little and often" being the method to follow. They should not be taken for rearing till covered with feathers and nearly ready to fly. The young of insectivorous birds of the smaller and more delicate kinds are best reared on white ants and small grasshoppers; of the larger, on egg-and-*satoo* paste and bread-and-milk, with whatever large insects come to hand. The young of seed-eaters need to be fed on paste and sop like those of insectivorous birds, not being able to digest hard seed till fledged. A small pair of forceps is the best thing for feeding young birds with; failing these, a quill toothpick with the tip rounded off answers very well. Drops of water must not be forgotten. Hand-reared birds generally become delightfully tame, and may in some cases be allowed complete liberty when able to look after themselves. This of course is the very best way of keeping tame birds, though not often possible.

Breeding.

All that can be done for breeding birds is to get true pairs and put them into roomy quarters with suitable nesting accommodation, and to supply food as natural as possible. Then if the species is naturally a free breeder, success will follow. As a general rule, more than one pair of the same species should not be put up for breeding in the same aviary, and their companions should not be birds of nearly related species.

When the sexes are alike in plumage, it is very difficult to pick out a true pair; but as a general rule males have larger and particularly longer heads and bills than females; and this slight difference of feature is all one has to go by.

Insectivorous birds and many Finches will often only feed their young on live food; and most Finches eat and require soft food when rearing young. It need scarcely be added that breeding birds should not be disturbed or looked at.

Taming wild-caught Birds.

A newly-caught bird should be placed in a cage covered all over, but not so as to darken it. Various kinds of seed and fruit should be strewn on the floor if it is a seed-eater, and decapitated insects if it is insectivorous. It will soon begin to feed if let alone for a day, and then, if it is a soft-food eater, the insects and fruit can be mixed with soft food to get it used to this. The perch should run from end to end in a cage used for taming birds, so that, when the front is uncovered as the bird eats well, it always looks its owner in the face, and sees that he feeds it. Thus it will acquire some confidence, and soon get tame if not incautiously approached or frightened.

Handling Birds.

Most ordinary cage-birds, like Finches or Parrots, should be held gently by the neck, this being passed between the fore and middle fingers with a small bird, the body lying in the palm of the hand. In this position the bird is quite helpless, and cannot hurt itself. In handling Parrots care must be taken to get a good hold, or the bird will manage to bite; a cloth over the hand is useful. Doves must be taken in the hand bodily; their necks are too slender and delicate to hold them by especially considering the strength of their wings used in resistance. If it be desired to open a bird's beak to make it swallow food, &c., this should be done by prizing it open at the side near the root, with some blunt flat instrument; or the bird, if not possessed of a formidable beak, may be induced to bite one's hand. Birds should never be handled or caught if it can be avoided, but if tame enough to be touched they much enjoy having their heads tickled. If they have to be caught in a large cage or aviary a hand-net should be used; or a quite small bird may be douched with water.

Diseases and Accidents.

If birds are given plenty of room, kept clean, and suitably fed, they will practically never be ill; but if under these circumstances, they do get out of sorts little or nothing can be done. At the same time cases occasionally happen which can easily be set right by simple treatment. The bill and claws, for instance, often overgrow, and should in such cases be cut back to their proper length with a sharp pair of scissors. A hen bird when breeding may suffer from egg-binding—be unable to lay her egg; in this case a little oil applied to the vent with a feather will probably give relief. A broken leg, if the fracture be a clean one, may be bound up with splints made from a quill, that being the method recommended by Dr. A. G. Butler.

To avoid disease and accidents the great requisite is not to overcrowd and not to put strong and weak birds together. A bird, the size of a Canary, as noted in the treating of small cages, needs a square foot of floor-space, and this rule should be rigidly adhered to in stocking aviaries and large cages. Most people crowd far too many birds together.

Secondly, birds of different sizes should not be put together as a general rule, or there will be trouble sooner or later. Of course, this rule must be modified with reference to the strength of birds' bills; a strong-billed small species may be more than a match for one with a bigger body and smaller beak. Insectivorous birds, if large, have a carnivorous tendency and are particularly untrustworthy with smaller companions.

The Best Birds to Keep.

For a good large outdoor aviary there is nothing to beat a collection of large insectivorous and fruit-eating birds—Jays, large Mynahs and Babblers, Lories, Barbets, &c.; and these are all easily kept on simple food.

For a small verandah aviary, such birds as the Budgerigar, Java Sparrow, and Pekin Robin, will certainly give satisfaction; all these three can be kept together in a space about six feet square. The Budgerigar and Java should breed well in such a home. Very small birds, suitable for cages only a yard square, are the Avadavat, Japanese Munia, Zebra Finch, and Silverbill. These may be associated with Canaries in a small aviary. If it be desired to breed good-sized birds, the Collared and Crested Doves, Rosella Parakeet and Cockatiel, will be found suitable tenants for a large aviary.

For song the Shama and Peko are most to be recommended to the beginner, unless he is satisfied with Canaries.

Transport of Birds.

It may very well happen that an amateur in India may wish to send or take some birds home, and I have been careful to indicate which species are rare enough there to be worth shipment. For sea transport birds need not be allowed so much room in their cages as is necessary in the case of a permanent habitation, though the more space they have the better. These cages should be of the box pattern, wired only in the front, and should have for a floor a wicker grating above the draw-tray, as this is a cleaner arrangement than the sanded tray when space and time are limited. Of course in this case some gravel should be supplied in a food-pot. Green food should also be occasionally given to birds on board ship; to delicate insectivorous species it is usually possible to give cockroaches as live food. If none can be had, pellets of minced washed raw meat should be given occasionally, but not too liberally, lest scouring be caused. The larger insectivorous species are much hardier in this respect, and are easy to manage.

Of course the best time to take birds home is in the hot weather; but too much heat in the Red Sea is a disadvantage, though not so dangerous as the winter's cold further on.

Birds on board ship are usually looked after by the butcher, who should of course be propitiated by a substantial "tip." As the charge of freight on birds—in the P. & O. at all events—is one pound per ordinary-sized cage, it is obvious that a single bird is not worth taking home, unless a decided rarity or a much-prized pet.

INDEX.